TALES FROM THE
Whispering
BASKET

An exhilarating collection of short stories and poetry

Larry Spotted Crow Mann

Edited by Donna Caruso

ISBN: 1461013054
ISBN-13: 9781461013051

Cover art by Michelle Vigeant
Interior Photos –Licy Mann & Amber Rubidoux
Back cover Photo - Curtis Cleaves
whisperingbasket.com

Preface

❦

Tales *from the Whispering Basket* is an excellent selection of short stories and poetry by Nipmuc Tribal member of Massachusetts, Larry Spotted Crow Mann. He draws on his Native American roots, but also delivers magnificent tales that transcend all walks of life. This captivating collection will take the reader on an epic journey of adventure and wonder that will surely stimulate a mosaic of passions! His story **Deal Me In** is based on a story of love and unity that was formerly passed down orally in his family for many generations and gives you a taste of his tribe's past and present. Demonstrating the author's flexibility to reach beyond roots and into the soul of Everyone, **Soul Inspiration** reflects contemporary problems such as overcoming loneliness and finding romance – but, with some unexpected bumps in the road. Mann bases his historical novella **Mattawamp** on the actual Nipmuc Chief and hero to Massachusetts Natives whose life culminated in the events of King Phillip's War. When Nipmucs were being sold into slavery by the Commonwealth's governor, being systematically murdered, having their land stolen, and forced into Christian

Praying Towns, Mattawamp fought back. Mann's account, beginning during the time that Mattawamp is fourteen years of age, represents a long overdue resurrection of this warrior, dreamer, and leader. **Deadly Deeds** entertains but also triggers a roller coaster of excitement with its unexpected outcome. The tale of **The Basket** hits close to home to millions of Native Americans and is based on actual events and painful issues Native Americans continue to wrestle with; the story also reflects the power of the ancestors to help us heal. Mann's compilation of poetry in this volume reflects both this world and the places of dreams and nightmares. The writer lets you into those dark yet beautiful, horrible yet enjoyable, places of the mind and matter.

To All My Relations

Introduction

❀

*W*unne-Nog-Kishkoad-Tuonk! That is the Nipmuck phrase for "*Greetings, glad you're here!*" I want to truly thank you for taking the time to join me on this adventure. This book was put together not only to share my heart and soul but also to bring to light a translucent dream. There are things shared that transcend the physical existence and voyage into realms beyond the stars. My inner Spirit speaks loudly inside this work and amalgamates with experiences throughout my walk on this earth.

We are all human beings first. I happen to come from the First Nations People of the Nipmuck Tribe of Massachusetts. Certainly growing up as Native American shaped my life in ways I was not always prepared for or even appreciated. But the inherent connection to this land and the teachings from the Elders has been the grounding force that permeates my life.

That's why it's important to point out: the aesthetics of our tradition and culture are sacred and beautiful but many people are not aware of the painful daily realities we face as Native people. Struggles and difficulties are a part of every society but the unique perspective we Indians have to this country can't be ignored. America is a marvelous and wondrous country that was made at the expense, removal, and murder of millions of Indians that were here first. That inescapable reality sorely reveals itself in many facets of Native American life today. From issues of Sovereignty to disproportionate poverty, loss of tribal lands, and ongoing governmental changes and regulations that tend to have deleterious effects on the daily lives of Native peoples everywhere.

However, by no means is there a dismal outlook for the future of Native Americans. If anything, Indians have shown the resilience and strength to move forward against the odds and not only recover, but to take an active and leading role in our own self-determination. Education, tradition, ceremony, and following the path of the Elders is our path to recovery. We may have not had control of the past, but with the growing number of Native American scholars, writers, directors and entrepreneurs, and most of all Spiritual Leaders, we can script our own future.

Conversely, I must say, my book is not solely about reflecting the story of Native Americans. It delves into the primordial connection we all have as creatures of this world and challenges our way at looking at things we perceive. As I said above, we are all human beings first. We don't have a choice in our ethnic background or the color of our skin. But as human beings we do have a choice in how we interact with one another.

On a note on diction, you may notice the spelling of Nipmuc or Nipmuck throughout the reading. The Nipmuck community has several thousand citizens. Certain clans and families use either one of these spellings. I chose to use both.

The Title: I wanted to do my best to capture the essence and flavor of what I present in this writing. Baskets are a precious commodity to Nipmuck people; they were used to chronicle our days and clanship. Also they served the practical purpose of storing important and sacred items of our Tribes. In addition they were used for trade as a way for our people to survive. In short, the Basket was a way for Nipmucks to provide for their families and carry on culture and tradition. And out of that Basket is everything I share in this book, which is stimulated by the mosaic and reverberation of the infinite universe. The Basket represents the creativity and beauty of life all around us.

With the five stories I sought to challenge my creativity as well as share things that are dear to me. They are all special and bring forth their own message that I hope you enjoy.

Deal Me In: This tale was based on stories my mother and grandmother use to share with us when we were children. It's about family, love and unity. I think you'll find this story very interesting and precious.

Soul Inspiration: This is a story that I thought about writing for years. I saw the entire account in my mind and all that needed to be done was to write it down. This story has a theme of overcoming loneliness and finding love, but with a few bumps in the road.

Deadly Deeds: This narrative is my shortest story and I wanted to harness all the emotion, energy and mood in as few words as possible.

Mattawamp: This reading is based on the real life Nipmuck Chief and hero of the King Phillip's War of 1675. It was Mattawamp who was the most brilliant military leader and Commander of the War. *(*King *Phillip's War, Schultz & Tougias 1999.)* Throughout the story, I diligently worked to reflect the accurate and historical relationship Nipmucks had with the English and other Tribes during the late 1600s. Nipmucks sacrificed and nearly lost everything because of this war but there's not a lot of information reflecting our history concerning this period. I think it's very important that one of the leaders who fought bravely to defend this land first be honored and remembered. When Nipmucks were being sold into slavery, murdered, lands usurped, forced into Christian Praying Towns, and Tribal tradition being decimated, Mattawamp fought back. My story takes you back many years before the war, when Mattawamp was 14 years old.

Come along on this epic journey as this young warrior deals with the changing world around him. With this narrative we bring Mattawamp back to life. The story represents a long overdue resurrection of an intrepid warrior, dreamer, and Leader of the Nipmuck People.

The Basket: This writing chronicles the journey of a sacred Nipmuc Basket and speaks to the real and painful issues facing Native people yesterday and today.

My Poems: These poems are a reflection of things of this world and other places my dreams and nightmares take me. I remove myself from this so-called lucid reality and go to some ineffable space; dark and beautiful. I get to see things in places I'm not sure where I'm at, occasionally I enjoy it, other times I'm horrified. A poem may carry a special meaning or speak to you in a way that only you understand. Life has many angles to it. But because we all look at it from different points, we may not feel the same edge.

Larry Spotted Crow Mann

Table of Contents

Deal Me In 1

Soul Inspiration. 11

Mattawamp .35

Deadly Deeds 73

The Basket 77

Poems

The Crow (In his own words) 95

Citrus Smile. .97

I've Been here before 99

Message from Mother Earth 101

Drove Past a Funeral Home Today 103

Dye for my Sin 105

Hearing Voices 107

I Love Pow Wow 109

Shatter Proof Heart 111

Edge of Sanity 113

Heart in the Clouds. 115

Downstairs Devil 117

Wounded Rain 119

Cerulean Skies. 121

Madness 123

Garbage Eater. 125

Sneaking into the Dream 127

Professor Profess 129

Melting Candle. 131

Remove 133

Pressing to the Womb. 135

Fool's Mask 137

The Hateful look 139

The Darkening. 141

My Words Mean Nothing 143

Deal Me In

☙❧

Early in the last century, in the 1930's, my mother's family lived in the woods of northeastern Connecticut in an area just shy of the Massachusetts border. The land was rich with wildlife and dotted with clean lakes full of fish. Streams meandered through lush forests without dams or mills. Only narrow footpaths and dirt roads just wide enough for a single, occasional horse-drawn buggy interrupted the old-growth forests.

Carved out of the heart of the mixed oak, ash, pine and birch woodlands, and nearly hidden among them, were six cabins clustered within a half square mile of one another. This is where my grandparents, aunts and uncles farmed, fished, hunted, and otherwise lived off the land. This was their home, as well as the home of our ancestors, since time immemorial.

Mother Earth provided everything they needed, so my grandparents rarely had to go into town. These houses weren't perfect or as good as our ancestors' longhouses or *wetus,* but the people did their best with the cabins. For instance, leaky roofs were a problem from time to time and some of the local critters could get inside and take a meal for themselves.

Clean, cold running water was outside at the well near the corn field. Kerosene lamps provided light, especially needed when walking to the outhouse in the dark of night. Grandma told us that one of the best memories of their cabin was the stone fireplace. The pleasant scent of cedar, coupled with the sound of crackling embers added an inviting touch to their home. So warm, cozy, and peaceful did she feel that just sitting near its warmth would bring her good Medicine. She would snuggle into her quilt for hours, listening to stories from her Elders of great mysteries and wondrous happenings, as well as life lessons to guide her.

The work was hard but everybody pitched in. They enjoyed life and took care of one another. Because of this they were fearless. No one ever had the need to talk about the Great Depression because their sharing allowed them to survive and the atmosphere around them was that of tenderness and joy.

One thing about Indian people is that they know how to have a good time and laugh; even when life is at its toughest. So, once a week, ever since anyone could remember, my grandmother said that the entire family would all gather at Uncle Henry's cabin for the weekly card game. Now, Uncle Henry, like my Great Grandma, knew how to use herbs, roots, and trees of the forest to cure and heal ailments. He was also connected to the Sprit World and would share stories and songs about our relatives from the past with the help of the family Drum. After Great Grandma crossed over to the Land of Endless Spirits they all relied on Uncle Henry for most of the healing.

Uncle Henry was tall – over six feet, and his skin was light brown like an autumn oak leaf. He combed his straight black hair back and it reached all the way to his shoulders.

He was always smiling and was known as one of the nicest people you could ever meet. That's probably why the weekly card game was always at his place: he would never say 'no' to it and never yelled at anyone about the mess left behind.

Of course, you can't have a card game without a feast to go with it. Everyone brought a little something. Some of their favorites, depending on the season, were venison stew, succotash, corn-on-the-cob, fiddleheads, baked beans, and corn cake topped with wild berries. And of course there was plenty of bannock bread and coffee to last the people throughout the evening.

So on this particular day, as they have done since anyone can remember, my family held the weekly card game. All twelve of my folks played cards late into the night, laughing, eating, and joking with one another with friendly insults and jibes.

What a beautiful sight it must have been, and how glad I am that they told me all about it. Imagine! All my relatives sitting around that worn-down pine table in the kitchen. One of the legs was off by about two inches and some of the old playing cards from years past were stuck underneath it to bring back its balance. The kitchen was very simple and rustic, no finished or stained wood there. Sturdy, handmade cabinets were mounted by the ice box and over the window sill. A wooden barrel of flour rested by itself in the corner, lonely looking except everyone knew its friendly contents. The shelves were home to *Nipmuc* storage baskets made by Uncle Paul and Aunt Hanna. Some had tobacco; some held herbs and others, natural remedies that Uncle would use. The small, wood-burning stove sat by the back door so as soon as you walked in, you would be captured by the aroma of the stew or bannock bread being turned in the cast iron pan by an aunt. And the back plate on the stove was a permanent home for that old aluminum coffee pot.

Every now and then a relative would get up to grab some more bannock or go into the living room to stoke the fire to curb the chill from the spring air. That night, as Uncle Billy put another log in the fire, he complimented his brother Henry for his fine workmanship on the hand-carved bows and arrows that were mounted on the wall to the left of the fire place next to the fishing and hunting supplies and more split-ash baskets.

Even though the game got intense at times, it was all in good fun. Uncle Paul would be 'up' in the game and always thought he was the best player anyhow. Once in awhile he would send playful taunts to his wife Aunty Hanna to catch up. Uncle John and Aunt Nellie were very competitive and were working together on a strategy to out-do Paul. Uncle Billy would lose track of his hand sometimes because he would be re-telling the family how he caught the biggest fish in the world. Aunt Doris and the rest of them struggled to keep up but still had fun. They never played for money, but they played with just as much vigor and excitement as if a lot of money was at stake. Uncle Henry didn't even care if he won or not, he was just always happy to have his family with him and to be surrounded by so much love.

Then out of nowhere there was a weird knock at the door. It was strange because everyone around there just walks in and says 'hello'. The nearest town was 20 miles away and it was 11:30 at night and nobody comes around after dark in those parts. The forest was so dark you couldn't see your hand in front of you. The knock caused a sudden pause from the laughter and chatter. The flame from the kerosene lamp by the window jumped back from the unexpected thump. Even the crickets and peepers outside took a momentary interlude from their singing. All the eyes in the kitchen abruptly turned to the door, then to each other in a nervous grin sort of fashion. They were all wondering who it could be.

Uncle John had a rushing thought to himself that maybe it was the Indian Affairs Agency coming to try and take their land. Aunt Doris reflected on similar fears that state agents were coming to rip away the children and ship them off to Carlisle Indian Boarding School.

Uncle Henry quickly sensed the unease in his family and said, "Ok, everybody. Let's relax. It's gonna be fine; let me just see who it is." When he opened the door, there stood a very handsome, well dressed white man. He was over six feet tall, with a clean shaven face that highlighted his placid, soft features and he looked about 30 years old. His blue eyes perfectly matched his neatly pressed shirt which in turn blended nicely with his white, silk bow tie. Black suspenders fettered to his dark pinstripe pants neatly embraced his well-shined Spectator shoes. He carried a finely made brown-suede satchel over his left shoulder. Neatly combed, sandy brown hair was revealed when the man removed his black fedora hat. As he tipped his hat to Uncle Henry, the man unleashed a huge, white smile and said in a crisp, robust voice, "Good evening, sir. I was just passing through and I overheard all the laughter, joy, and love coming from this cabin and I just knew I had to stop in!"

Uncle Paul yelled out, "Sorry mister, we don't want what you're selling. If ya keep movin,' ya should make it to town by daybreak!" Uncle Henry cut in saying, "Now Paul, that's not our way." Turning to the stranger, he said, "What can we do for you, sir?" The man said, "Oh gosh, no, I'm not selling anything! I'm just passing through, would you invite me in for a respite?"

Henry gave an affirmative nod and said, "Sure come on in, welcome to our home." The man then walked through the back door and stood by the wood stove as everybody got up and introduced themselves. As the family went back to their chairs to resume the game, the man's eyes beamed around the house taking notice of every little detail. He looked so intense at their belongings and the order of things that it seemed to them that he was conducting a military-style barracks inspection. Henry made a peculiar and stern face as he watched the stranger scan his home–a glance no one had ever seen from him before. For a moment, Henry stared the stranger down–another unknown behavior to the family–but the next moment, his usual jovial smile returned and he asked "Would you like to join the game?" The Stranger responded with a big smile and replied, "Yes. Deal Me In!"

While the man pulled up a chair at a corner end of the table, Uncle Billy causally inquired, "Sir, what did you say your name was?" Instead of answering, though, the man reached into his satchel and pulled out a huge wad of cash. As he dropped it on the table, he said "OK, so how much we betting?" At this point Uncle Henry took the opportunity to explain to the man that his family doesn't play for money and that this game is more of a symbol of unity and family togetherness. While other relatives went around the table echoing the same sentiments, it seemed the question of the stranger's name was lost in the conversation.

With a loud chuckle, the stranger said "Oh, that's fine, fine." And he put the money away while adding, "Deal me in, I'll play any way you like!" The stranger went on to score the lowest hand, four games in a row. "Well now, I'm just not that good at the game you're playing so it looks to me that you folks could have won a pocket full of money!", he said while taking his money back out and waving it in the air. "It's not too late!" he declared.

Uncle Billy became annoyed with this line of talk and said, "Listen mister, we know your world, the white world, where you think you can buy and sell everything. That's not our Way. To us, some things are more important, like family, love and respecting Mother Earth!"

While still sporting that handsome smile the stranger shouted back. "Whoa! Whoa, there pal, hold your horses, I'm just offering … thought you folks could use a few bucks." The leader of the family offered some words. "Ok, everyone, let's calm down and have a good time. We do have a guest and he will be treated as such." The stranger replied, "Why thank you, Henry. I suppose I do understand. After all that you folks have been through, I bet you just hate white people and wish they all be dead, right? Right?" Henry said, "Well, sorry sir, but you're wrong again. Hate only breeds hate, and darkens the hearts of those who allow it to rule their life."

As the card game resumed, the stranger's face took a more serious and harsh appearance. He won the next hand, and then the next. Almost two hours went by and he hadn't lost a hand. Then he barked out in a voice much deeper than before, "Guess you're not as good as you thought, Paul!" Of course Paul was instantly wondering what would make the stranger say that because how could he know of the bravado he always proclaimed at the card table since they never saw him before.

Things were getting eerie to say the least. Who was this man and how could he be winning every hand? The stranger smugly said, "Pretty sad bunch you are, losing like that in your own home." Uncle Henry smiled in the face of the man's criticism and replied, "No, sir. We already won. Having all this love and sharing with one another is winning to us." The stranger appeared to snarl at the comment then came back with his own thoughts while reaching back into his satchel. "Golly that's great! Speaking of sharing, I'd like to share with all of you this swell jug of whisky!" The family looked back and forth at each other coupled with an expression as if they'd bitten into a sour apple. The stranger then said loudly, "Com' on boys and girls! This ain't your typical swamp yankee mash. I brought you folks the good stuff. Drink up!!"

"Whisky!? Nobody drinks alcohol here!" Uncle Billy asserted; "Years ago, I was the only one in the family who drank that poison. I gave it up. It's a killer! Put it away!" Uncle Henry noticed the rising tension and stepped in. "Please sir, we ask that you respect our wishes and put the alcohol away. As my brother told you, we don't drink and it's not allowed in our home. Our well water is the sweetest in these parts; we also have some fine coffee if you wish?"

With a hard grin, the stranger remarked "Well, I humbly apologize, I was under the impression you folks were quite fond of the fire water. Please forgive my assumption. Shall we proceed with the game?" There remained unease in the room but things settled down for the moment. It was Aunt Doris' turn to deal the cards. In the midst of her passing the cards around, one flew off the table and landed underneath the stranger. Henry told her "Don't worry, I'll grab it." As he bent down under the table he made a startling discovery. The stranger's feet had turned into hooves and his legs resembled that of a deformed goat! Henry gasped at the scene but while still under the table he pulled himself together before resurfacing with the card.

Henry coolly put the card on the table. "Excuse me, everyone, I need to go check the fire." Uncle Henry calmly walked into the living room, out of sight of everyone in the kitchen. He walked in the direction of the fire place but then went past it toward the bow and arrow, baskets and hunting supplies on the wall. "Hey, Henry, you coming back in, we're waiting on ya," Aunt Helen called out. After about five minutes passed, Henry walked back to the kitchen. His hands were behind his back as if he was concealing something. He then went to the opposite end of the table and stood looking at the stranger in a serious way, but with a smile.

A few minutes went by but Henry maintained his posture. Just as the family began to openly express puzzlement, Henry spoke loudly to the man:

"*Teag-Kuk-Quen-Aue-Hik?*" (What do you want?)

The stranger blasted out a deep laugh and responded, "*Kutah-Toup Muppuhkik Wunne!*" (Ah! you are a wise man!) The stranger's *Nipmuc* was perfect!

"Who is this? Do we know you?" Aunt Helen asked in disbelief. Henry then told all his family to stay calm and that everything would be all right. He said to the stranger, "On behalf of me and my family, we want to thank you for stopping by. I know what you are and who you are. I suppose sooner or later, everyone will have to meet you and make a choice of what path to choose. As you see, my family isn't interested in what you have to offer and it's time for you to leave. *Amaish!*" The man became very sweaty and began loosening his bow tie. "What's your name, mister?" Paul asked in a stern voice.

Uncle Henry went on to say. "I'm sure he has many names. Our people call him The *Trickster*." The *Trickster* growled out at Henry saying "Fools, you're all a bunch of stupid fools!" Henry shouted back, "I said it's time for you to leave!" At that very same moment, Henry leapt at the *Trickster*. He called out a Nipmuc Prayer "*Wame –Masugkenuk Manitoo, Keen Notah!*" Revealing finally what was in his hands, he thrust their contents at the *Trickster*. A beautiful all-white eagle feather and sacred herbs from the Basket. The *Trickster* instantly began to heave as if choking on a large object. Then he fell back in his chair and landed on his back.

His hoofed feet and deformed goats' legs were therefore exposed before the room of people. With great haste, the *Trickster* jumped up and sped toward the back door, running on all fours! Then it barreled out the door, with its black gnarly tail the last thing they saw. It took off through the woods and to this day, our family does not deal in the *Trickster* when it comes knocking at the door.

⌘ ⌘ ⌘

Soul Inspiration

The rosy-cheeked, pleasant-looking emcee announced, "Good evening, ladies and gentlemen! Thank you for attending our Book Garden Awards at Chez Laval Plaza! Now – the moment we have all been waiting for – this year's winner of the Book Garden Award! An author of five best-selling novels! A winner of the 2005 Platinum Pen Award! A leading fundraiser for the Book Garden's Youth Foundation! Please! Give him a big welcome! Claude! Come on up here, Claude Young! Claude, we love ya!"

A handsome, physically-fit man of medium height walked to the Plaza's polished oak stage wearing a black, tailor-made tuxedo. Calmly smiling, he waved confidently to the crowd. Women, and certainly a few men, adored his black, wavy hair that sometimes fell across his deep-set brown eyes. Claude reached the podium, and surveyed the audience of 400 people. Sleek women in beautiful, formal summer gowns and handsome men in stylish tuxedos filled the hall and their clapping and whistles erupted in a loud din. Claude's presence became even more stunning to the audience as he stood, arms to his sides, below the crystal chandeliers; light from satin white table settings before him cast an even more star-quality glow around him.

Claude waited for the applause to subside and said, "Thank you! Thank you! Thank you, to the Book Garden Award Foundation for sponsoring this event. Moreover, thank you for the wonderful champagne!" A club member sitting in the back smiled and whispered a comment to another member: "The rich prick. He could buy an entire vineyard if he wanted."

Claude then said, more humbly, "I just want to say, fifteen years ago when I began writing, I wasn't sure how far I could go, but thanks to all of you, you made me number one. And moreover, the inspiration behind all my work is, and always has been, my lovely wife. Sarah!" The crowd smiled and applauded; few understood, though, the deep sincerity of Claude's praise for his wife, who was also perfect, with a beautiful smile and a light-blue dress delicately accented with hundreds of hand-sewn crystals. "I love you too, Claude," she shouted out to him, and blew him a kiss.

Across town, Rachael Moore sat alone in Nandy's Pub sipping her fourth rum and coke. Nandy's was a shabby sort of bar, but had a friendly, working-class atmosphere whose liberal bartenders provided a place for anyone to drink away whatever ailed them. Rachael was 27 years old, with a round face and full-figure who hated both her weight and her red hair. Sadly, she went through as many unlucky relationships as she had gone through failed diets. Her forlorn, hazel eyes seemed to radiate off the neon German beer light at the end of the bar, but then became blurred by the amber liquid that she swallowed, adding even more misery into her soul.

Rachael was a full-time teller at City Savings Bank. Ordinarily, she would deal with the sadness in her life by overeating: entire boxes of crème-filled chocolate-layered cookies, pints of locally-made, cream-top ice cream, late-night toasted bagels smeared with both peanut butter *and* butter. After her most recent disappointment, however, food was not enough. Heartbroken yet again, she needed and chose something more potent.

An orphan who was raised in foster homes, Rachael had been on an endless search for love and acceptance throughout her adult life. The only true love and friend she had growing up was her soft, cloth doll with its beautiful porcelain face. She admired the doll and took it everywhere. The doll was thin, yet cuddly, pretty yet accessible, and everything else that Rachael wished that she was but never would be.

Only six months before, Rachael met a man she thought was the man of her dreams. He showed her tremendous love and admiration. Dinners and movies were their normal routine. Romantic walks and picnics on the beach were activities she only dreamed about before but now were hers. Her lover would write her elegant poetry and even sang outside her window one night. Rachael was elated that she finally found love. Then this dreaded day came, the one that found her downing rum and cokes at Nandy's Pub. She shouted out in her high, slurred voice, "Another drink, please!" As she drank more pain-numbing fluid, she thought about what had happened earlier in the day.

She left City Savings early that morning and decided to surprise her lover with a visit and lunch. She ran up the stairs to his apartment with a bag from Tata's Deli. Her red hair and chest bounced with each step and her face resembled a child running toward the Christmas tree on the 25th. Catching her breath, she gave the door a little tap-tap. When there was no answer, she listened and heard loud noises in the distance. "Is that the TV?" she thought. After tapping again without results, she pulled out the key her boyfriend had given her months ago. She walked in. Some 1980s rock-and-roll classic video was blaring from the television throughout the apartment. She turned down the volume and called out her lover's name. Again, there was no answer but she did hear another noise, this time coming from the bedroom. She walked in just in time to see the girl her boyfriend was screwing pull up her panties and jump over the bed for her bra.

Like an electric jolt, Rachael's thoughts returned to her present moment at Nandy's. With a face covered in tears, she slammed her empty glass down and stumbled to the door. A man standing by the juke box tried to stop her and asked if she was all right. She responded to his question by slapping him hard across his face. "Mind your own fucking business!" she shouted and she staggered to her little blue Toyota and sped down the road.

Back at Chez Laval Plaza, Claude and Sarah had finished dinner while they engaged in polite conversation with dignitaries from the Book Garden. "I want to thank you again, Mr. Sullivan, for a fine evening." "No, Claude, thank *you;* and keep writing those books!" Claude and Sarah said their goodbyes. He tipped the valet generously for bringing around his red, convertible sports Mercedes. He waited for Sarah to be seated, and then allowed the valet to open his own door. As soon as Claude began to drive home, both husband and wife chatted easily about the evening. Claude said to his wife, "Well, my sweet, you should write your own book." "Book? What about, dear?" He gave her his most sincere smile and said, "You could write a book on what it's like to make love with the best writer in the world." "Hah! Wise ass," she said, smiling and elbowing his side "You're going to be doing a lot of writing, and you'll need your hand for more than holding your pen if you don't watch it!" Her words were accented by a sensuous smile.

As Claude drove the Benz along Route 20, Rachael's car approached. Intoxicated, with her radio blasting, and talking to herself while driving 60 mph in a 40 mile zone, she didn't correct her car when she veered to the wrong side of the road. "Why? God! *Why* does this keep happing to me? Do you hate me that much? I'm sick of this shit! I can't take it anymore!" She accelerated to 80 mph as her screaming and crying continued. Claude leaned over to give his beautiful partner a quick kiss. At the same moment that he turned his eyes back on the road, he saw the little blue Toyota rocketing at them.

Knock, knock, knock! The sound of a police officer knocking on Claude's car window snapped Claude back to the present moment. It was a dark, blue-lit night. The rain was coming down, cold and hard. Claude had sat in his car so long, lost in thoughts of the past that his windows were fogged over. He was parked in front of Chez Laval Plaza, the last place that he was happy, the final place he had wealth and fame, and the last place he and his wife had a good time just before she was killed. Rachael Moore died that night, too. His wife was killed instantly but Rachael lingered. Still in shock and injured himself, after he tended to his wife, Claude inexplicably ran to the car that had hit them. He saw a virtually unrecognizable woman behind the wheel. Covered in blood, shards of glass could be seen in her forehead. Her body was mashed between the seat and steering wheel. Her mangled arm reached out to Claude as if not asking for help, she knew she was beyond that, but reaching out for … love. She showed a pain on what was left of her face that transcended her physical torture. Claude, stunned, stayed with her in her remaining moments. As her last discernable life sign began to fade, people came running and screaming over from Cozy's Gas-N-Go Mart. To the sound of stranger's voices, Rachael's hazel eyes became totally coated in the blood.

That was six years ago. Claude lived alone in poverty now. He hadn't written anything since the night his wife was killed. "Hey! Claude!" the policeman who had knocked on his car window yelled. "You can't keep coming here. Why don't you go home?" Claude rolled down the window of his old, beat-up Plymouth Breeze. The trunk was held down by a bungee cord from the time he backed into a wall. The cop looked in the car and took in the dirt, chaotic mess, and cigarette butts covering the floor. Claude lifted his head, covered with an old, dirty baseball cap he wore to keep from having to comb his hair. His hooded eyes slowly shifted from the steering wheel to the policeman. He looked through the window at the officer with a sullen smile. "Go home? Home is where the heart is, eh officer?" Claude then picked up one of the half-smoked cigarettes from the floor and lit it. "Sure I'll go home." As he drove off, his body tensed with the now familiar effort to hold back tears. Just as his broken right wiper blade couldn't hold back the rain, neither could his body fight the gush.

For the first year after her death, Claude lived virtually next to Sarah's grave. He would bring flowers everyday, read to her, and talk as if she was still there. "Hey, honey, sorry I'm late today, these jerks from the bank keep calling our home. I told them I didn't have time to chat, me and the wife have a date tonight! So what do you want to wear? I brought you this hot little dress!" Every now and then one of the ground keepers would look at Claude and sadly shake his head. Some nights he would fall asleep next to her stone. He had been kicked out dozens of times. One of the grounds keepers walked over to Claude and said in a gentle voice, "Mr. Young, I'm sorry sir, but it's after hours and we have to lock the gates. You wouldn't want vandals to be here, now, would you?" Claude didn't respond, he just mournfully stared at his wife's gravestone with thoughts of happier times inter-twined with that deadly night. "Please sir, the last time I let you stay I got in trouble." Finally, Claude slowly stood up. "I'll see you tomorrow, darling" he said as he kissed the gravestone and then faded away.

After Claude sold their luxurious home, he couldn't bear to be in Reedsville. To get away, he bounced around the country and squandered their money. From Arizona to Maine and fourteen states in between, he wandered city streets, country sides, and parks. He spent two more years in Montreal, drinking, gambling, and staying in expensive hotels. While walking the Montreal streets, a prostitute would come up and put the moves on him from time to time. One night he was walking down Rue St. Catherine and a prostitute walked up to him. She wore a yellow bikini top and Daisy Duke short-shorts.

She said in a husky voice, "Bonjour mon beau, montre moi la tienne et je te montrerez la mienne!" He said, "Sorry I don't speak French" and as soon as he spoke, she stunned him by grabbing both of his arms and pulling him into an alley. She lifted her top and then attempted to heave his pants down but he was able to push her off and walk away. She laughed scornfully, lit a cigarette, and shouted French profanities. He suddenly froze, turned, and walked back to her. He stared at her for a moment as she stared back with a look of curiosity. Then he snatched the cigarette out of her mouth, smoked it himself, and slapped a fifty dollar bill in her hand before walking away.

Some days he would hang out in Old Montreal and listen to the street musicians. He would give the homeless ones money as well as buy them coffee and sandwiches at Tim Horton's. Other days he would simply sit at the pier along the St. Lawrence River and watch the boats and ships go by. Every now and then his attention would be turned to a young couple holding hands or laying in the grass kissing and looking at each other with adoring eyes. Claude found himself wandering, drifting away with thoughts of his wife

17

and all the good times they had. Then he turned back to the river and felt himself drowning within his own sorrow.

With his money almost gone and his spirit twisted and still wounded, he returned to Reedsville. Now virtually broke and barely getting by, he moved into a cheap one-bedroom on the third floor above Nandy's Pub. It was only a short drive to Chez Laval Plaza, so he could visit the last place he and his wife were happy. The last place he had wealth and fame. On the other hand, one place he never wanted to be near was Cozy's Gas-N-Go Mart.

After the police officer asked him to move along, he returned to his rundown apartment above Nandy's. He walked up to his door and stared as if he was a stranger or afraid to go in, or was afraid of more loneliness on the other side. Once inside, he took his usual position at the cracked, coffee-stained table in the small, gloomy kitchen. It was a lonesome table with a single wooden chair by the window; the only thing on it was a glass ashtray overrun by cigarette butts. He sat, holding his head in his hands, for more than thirty minutes. He finally looked up and out the window. He stared down at the people coming in and out of the Pub. The sound of laughter and friendly conversation accompanied the patrons as they rushed in to avoid the rain. He got up and walked to his little 'fridge to get the half-beer that was left in it. The 'fridge was empty as his life, except for the stale bread and box of mac-n-cheese. He took his beer to the living room that had a small used couch, CD player, coffee table, and a TV that he never used. He put on the only CD he owned: *Moonlight Sonata.* He reached under the coffee table where there were pictures of him and his late wife. He clinched one to his chest and danced around the room as if holding her. He then suddenly stopped, and melted into the sofa as he stared at his beloved with a look of joy and melancholy. He fell asleep on the couch as he regularly did with *Moonlight Sonata* playing on loop. He slept until 11 am.

The closest friend he had lived below him and was also his landlord. He stopped by once a month to say hello and collect the rent. Knocking continuously without a result, his friend shouted, "Hey Claude, I know you're there! It's the 12th and I haven't got the rent yet. Hello, Claude. Hello!" Claude walked to the door rubbing his eyes and said "Oh, hello Frank." Frank said, "Claude! Buddy, how are you, man?" Claude bent a little due to the weight of the 265 pound, 6' 4" landlord tapping him on the shoulder. Just after he coughed, he replied, "Ah, well, you know, taking it day by day," Frank said. "Listen, Claude, you gotta get some fun out of life! I mean, look at me! I got a belly so big I can't even see my pecker and that only works part time. My old lady says my gas is so bad she wants to fumigate my ass with pine sol!" Claude put his head down, holding in a smile, and said, "Uh … Frank" Frank cut back in and said "No, no, Claude, it's okay because see, I may have a bad case of gas but her ass is so big each cheek has its own zip code! Can you imagine an ass that big in your snout every night? Holy dog shit!" As Frank burst into robust laughter mixed with uncontrollable gagging, he changed the subject. "See pal, you gotta just make the best with what you got. Now, I'm gonna tell ya like I told you last month, I want you to hook up with my sister. She's got almost ten months clean and she'll be getting out of rehab in three weeks. I think she'll kick it this time. She digs all those books you wrote and I think you and her will hit it off!" Claude said, "Umm, uuh, thanks Frank, but I don't think I'm ready." Frank said, "Ok, she ain't gonna wait forever, you know. By the way, you got the rent?" Claude shuffled about in his place a bit and returned to the door. "Gee, Frank, all I have right now is Canadian money. I'm waiting for a residual check to come in but …." Frank interrupted, saying "Hey don't worry about it, but in the meantime you can go to the bank and exchange it! By the way, when you gonna write again?" Claude's face turned cold and he said, "I'm done writing. Thanks, Frank. I'll see ya."

Claude cleaned himself up and went to City Saving Bank to exchange the money. He walked into the bank and went up to a young, male teller. The teller was tall and slim and wore a satin purple shirt. His hair was gelled and combed back flawlessly. He had a beautiful face and perfectly groomed eyebrows. "Well, hello there darling, what can I do for you today?" he said seductively to Claude, who half-smiled and appeared to want to say something but was silent. The teller said, "Oh, don't mind me! I call everybody 'darling'. Plus, don't worry, I'm already taken!" Claude responded more quickly, "Uh no, it's not that ... it's ... could you exchange this currency please?" "Why sure!" As the teller made the exchange, Claude said, with a little more animation, "Whoa, you guys have great AC in here!" The teller tossed Claude a smile and wink and said, "Yeah, it *is* cold in here today, but you can come back when you feel hot. Have a nice day!" The teller in the next lane hurled over a comment, "*Travaughn, you're such a flirt!*" Claude left the bank, dropped the rent off with Frank, and then headed to Manixit Park.

It was a beautiful, warm, sunny day at the park. Birds swapped stories in the trees and bright yellow bumble bees kept busy smooching flowers. Parents played with their children on the swings and slides. Teens played basketball and volleyball. Claude found a comfortable bench alongside a path that led to the lake. He was feeling pretty good today; better than he had felt in a long time. As he soaked up the sun and threw bread to the crows, four guys who looked to be in their forties headed down to the lake for a swim. They were very loud and had obviously been drinking. As they headed past Claude, one man yelled, "I told him to go fuck himself if he thinks I'm working overtime and … hey – I know you – aren't you that big-shot writer guy?" Seeing the men were belligerent, Claude tried to ignore them. Then one of the men got in Claude's face. "Hey! Bud! I'm talking to you!" Claude put his head down and quietly said, "Yes, yes that was me, that was a long time ago, I don't write anymore." The man rubbed his chest and said "You hear that boys? He don't write anymore! Well my ex-wife thought you were awesome, but I told her YOU SUCK!" The man looked Claude up and down and said "Well. Boy, do you still *suck*?" The man stepped back and gave his buddies high fives as they all laughed. Claude took the opportunity to make his exit "Excuse me guys, I have to go." The most inebriated man in the group said, "What, you're too much of a big shot to hang out with us? Hah, fucker?"

Claude replied angrily, "No, it's just that I left pieces of shit like you in the toilet this morning." As Claude started to walk away, two of the men grabbed him and a third punched him in the stomach. Claude keeled over in the fetal position on the ground, coughing and gasping. He then jumped up and leapt at the men. Just as he charged in, he got punched in the face and went down again. Two of the men picked him up, then the one who recognized him said, "See, fucker, I told you, you suck!" Claude spat in his face and the man gave him a straight right to the nose and Claude crumbled to the ground again. Then one of them said, "Let's get out of here before the cops come!"

Claude rolled around on the ground for a few minutes in excruciating pain. When he got up, he felt his face and could tell that he had a busted lip, scraped face, bloody nose, and that his eyes would surely become black. He walked gingerly back to his car, slowly got in and looked at his busted face in the rearview mirror. As he drove off he knew he needed some bandages and peroxide. The nearest store, though, was

Cozy's Gas-N-Go Mart. Despite dreading the place, he didn't want to go back to his apartment and have Frank and people from the Pub see him, so he went anyway. He drove into the store parking lot, looked around, took a deep breath, and walked into the typical convenience store with over-priced products, odd gadgets and needless souvenirs. He found the first aid products that he needed as he walked past the beer holder hats and cheap, freeze-dried noodles.

As he decided what to buy, an inquisitive nine year-old boy stared at him. With just as much emphasis as his glare, he made a sudden comment. "You're all dirty, your face is dirty – you're bleeding – did you get beat up or something?" Claude bent close to the boy's ear. "Well, you know what?" he said to the boy. "I was in the park today and some apes and bears escaped from the zoo. They were attacking everybody – people everywhere were screaming and yelling! Then one huge ugly ape went after this little boy and I jumped in just in time to fight him off with my bare hands!" The boy's mouth was wide open and his eyes large as silver dollars. The boy said, "Wooow, that's coool!" But just as the boy spoke his mother yanked him away from Claude. She whispered loudly as she dragged him to the front of the store. "What did I tell you about that!?" The boy replies "Maaaa! I want candy! Gimme candy! You promised! Maaa!" As the boy's cries for candy faded away, Claude resumed his search for items to repair his face. He reached down to a lower shelf and found what he needed; as he turned around to leave, a woman stood in front of him. Immediately, they locked eyes. Time suddenly stopped for Claude as he stared at her. She had a glowing smile that lit up the store. She had a wholesome, natural beauty that took his breath away. Her hair was long and shiny like black liquid and her eyes were a dark brown that angled her soft face perfectly. He took in her medium height and slender build. Slim boot-cut jeans and a pearl-studded, off-white tight ribbed sweater showed off her curves, but in a modest way. Her presence gave Claude a rush through his soul that he hadn't felt in years. Then, in a voice that was like the sweetest melody he ever heard, she said, "Oh-excuse me!" Frozen, Claude continued to block her path but eventually he came to his senses. "Yes, oh ya, sorry –sorry, excuse me!" As she walked by, she turned back to him briefly and pitched Claude a delicate, warm smile. Claude, more than a little disoriented from this ordeal as well as his beating, managed to pull himself together and complete his purchase. He drove back to his place with his mind spinning with enthrallment for the woman in the store. "Who was *that*," he repeatedly asked no one, as he drove. "*Who* was that?"

After taking a long shower, he fixed up his face, popped in *Moonlight Sonata,* and stretched out on the couch with an ice pack on his head. But, listening as he had hundreds of times before, this time he was distracted and couldn't get the woman out of his thoughts. The next morning came, and for the first time, he found it difficult to go through his dismal routine. After pacing back and forth the whole afternoon like a caged animal, he decided to take a ride to Cozy's in order to, just by chance, see her again.

With his nicest clothes on, clean shaven and hair neatly combed, he probed the aisles for twenty minutes. "You need help with something, sir?" A squeaky, pubescent voice blurted out from the kid behind the counter. The kid wore an ancient Bob Marley tee shirt, a dirty hemp rope necklace and blond dreads. "No, I'm fine, thanks" Claude responded. To keep from looking like he was casing the store, he grabbed the first thing he saw. It turned out to be one of those stupid beer-holding hats. The only thing more disappointing than wasting $15.00 on the dorky booze cap was that the woman didn't show up. As soon as he walked out the door, the hat hit the trash. As he stood in front of his car fishing for his keys, though, he heard a voice that gave him chills. "Hope you're not fighting apes and bears again today!" He turned around and simultaneously swallowed the lump in his throat. "Ha ha, No I was just uh..." She put her hand out and said, "Hi, I'm Linda Ramos!" He was engulfed and en-raptured by her presence. She had the sweet smell of life and her spell-binding brown eyes looked at him for a thousand years. As their hands became one, the infusion of energy was an immediate spark that ignited Claude's universe. "I'm uh, Claude, Claude Young!" As her smile competed with the sun she said, "I recognized you... the writer! Five books! Oh, my favorite was *Dawn of the Shadow!*" Claude modestly chuck-led, "You read that?" "Yup! Sure did! That was some great stuff! What do you have out now?" Claude looked away and said, "Thanks very much, well I don't do that anymore"

She said, "Well, you should, it sure beats hanging around gas stations trying to pick up girls!" Claude blushed. "No, but I ... I bought this hat and ..." As Claude sifted through the trash to retrieve the Hick Head Gear, she stopped him. "Ha, ha, no-no I was just kidding. But actually, I'm new in town, I just moved into a place over on Pinecrest and don't know anyone. Do you think you could show me around a bit?"

Claude looked at her with a deep smile and replied, "Well, I think I filled my quota for gas station pick-ups for today!" They both laughed and then sat on the bench outside Cozy's for almost three hours chatting. Immediately Claude felt comfortable talking with her, as if she was a long lost friend. He informed her all about his life and loss of his wife. He revealed the tragic comedy his existence has been and the endless loneliness he has been experiencing for the last six years. That is, until now. She took Claude's hand, "Well, you never know when your life's gonna turn around for the better. It's getting kinda late, why don't I come to your place in the morning and you can show me around?" Claude replied, "That's a great idea, can't wait to see you ... I mean show you around!"

The next day Linda is at Claude's bright and early. "Good Morning! You ready to start our journey?" Claude said, "Absolutely!" She took Claude's hand and they headed down the stairs. Frank was just returning from the pharmacy with a liter of Anti Gas liquid in his hand. "Boy! You're up early!" Frank said. Claude replied, "Good Morning to you, too, Frank!" As he squeezed past Frank, the two new friends headed out on their adventure. "Ok, Linda, put your seat belt on!" "I always do!" she said back. Claude drove off and into a state of complete bliss. He took her around Reedsville which only took an hour but the tour turned into three weeks of them spending every day together. Laughing, talking, sharing their hopes and dreams, they were totally captivated by each other.

Claude was very nervous but he decided to take the relationship to the next level. As he was about to drop her off at her place he said, "It's been such a pleasure and joy spending these days with you, I can't remember the last time I felt so good. Would you like to go dancing and have dinner tomorrow night?" Her eyes sparkle to the inquiry. "I was wondering when you were gonna ask, but how about we have a quite romantic dinner and dance at your place?" Claude said, "Yes, that would be great! I'll see you tomorrow about 8 pm?" She replied "You got it!"

The following morning, Claude got up at 6 am. He cleaned his apartment from top to bottom, went out and bought a second chair and another CD: Miles Davis' *Blue in Green*. He also got a crimson-colored tablecloth to hide the table stains and a glass candle holder for a new center piece. After buying some new clothing, he sped off to Anoki's Catering to order two gourmet seafood dinners. "Can you please deliver them exactly at 7:50 pm tonight?" The chef said "Sure thing, sir!" He got back to his place, popped in Miles Davis, and glided around the apartment as he prepared for the greatest night of his life. Before he knew it, it was 7:35 pm. Knock! Knock! "Wow, the food's early!" Instead of being greeted with crab-stuffed lobster, roasted garlic and herb shrimp with bow-tie pasta, lightly buttered broccoli florets and Anoki's best champagne, there stood Frank. "Hey ya, Claude, I've been thinking about ya and, well ... my sis is out of rehab and she would love to meet ya." Claude quickly replied "Frank! Frank! You jolly Nipmuc giant!" Claude grabbed Frank by the hands and waltzed him around the kitchen and said "Thanks so much Frank, but I'm in looove! I found someone, that gorgeous gal you've seen me with!" Frank seemed to show disappointment and said, "Well, okay Claude, have a great night."

Just as Frank left, the delicious food arrived and Claude lit the candle at the center of the table. Another few minutes later, there was another knock at the door. He restarted Miles Davis, braced himself and walked to the door. When he opened the door there stood a work of majestic art. Linda was wearing a silk, black lace dress. It gently hugged and accentuated her petite but packed curves. The delicate and deep V chiffon overlay design around her chest conveyed mystery but yet ecstasy. The top of her radiant hair was twisted and wrapped in a mouth-watering bun, while the back was made into heavenly waves that softly retreated like a sensuous ebony waterfall to her breasts. Claude was paralyzed by her beauty but reached deep inside to be as cool as possible and make the evening wonderful. Then in all his coolness and Mr. Davis cheering him on, he spoke. "You look nice, come on in!" They sat down and had a scrumptious dinner while Miles did his thing in the background.

"What a wonderful dinner! How did you put all this to-gether?" Linda asked. Claude answered, "Well it's my favorite recipe. It's called *Crevettes- par-Anoki.*" They both burst into laughter. "Well, Mr. Young, you're gonna have to give me the recipe"

"Sure thing, Miss Ramos. It's $59.99 a plate." he said as the laughing continued. She then gave Claude a profound and thoughtful look. "You know, you should write again!" Without hesitation he said, "Ah, I don't know, I don't think I have it in me. I don't know what to write anymore." She urged, "Yes you do it's all in there; all your experiences, your life! Don't try to force it, just relax and write with your heart. Whatever pain or suffering you ever felt put it on paper. It will do you good as well. Some of those wild adventures and people you met in Montreal – write about it!" Claude stared at her and seemed to drift away with his thoughts for a moment but then returned to Linda. "Ok I'll think about it." They finished up dinner and took their champagne into the living room. "Would you dance with me, Linda?" She gazed into his eyes, wrapped her arms around his neck as he embraced her tight to his body. They were both swept away in their own little galaxy as they swayed to the soft rhythms and orbited the old grey sofa. On their sixth turn they made a smooth landing on the couch. They lay snugly next to each other and Linda rested her head under Claude's neck. He turned to face her as she looked up at him and their two mouths came together. It's was a long, hot, sizzling kiss that led his tongue on a path to her neck then down to her chest. His hands caressed her thighs and traversed her hips. He worked methodically up to her breast, then deli-cately stroked her neck, kissing her behind the ears, slowly removing her dress. She unpinned the rest of her hair and it surged out like the universe and Claude felt weightless. She took off his shirt and began to kiss his stomach, working her way back up to his mouth. Her hands cupped tightly around his throbbing and pulsating chest that pounded to the beat of her love. She stood, with only her fiery red silhouette lace panties and strapless bra on. Linda then walked Claude by the hand into the bedroom. She laid him down and straddled him. Claude touched her face and said, "I love you, Linda, I love you so much." She caressed his lips and stroked his hair and said, "I've been waiting so long for you, I love you, too, Claude. Forever, forever!" They make passionate love throughout the night. And for the next three days both remained there in the apartment.

They make more passionate love, laugh, share stories and build a loving bond that seals their spirits as one. As they're having breakfast, Claude made an announcement. "Ok, Linda, I'll do it!" Surprised, she asked, "Do what?" Claude answered back with, "I'm going to write again! And – will you marry me?" She jumped up and said, "Hurry-yay! And of course I'll marry you!" This was followed by big kisses and Linda jumped into his arms with her legs wrapped around him. Claude carried her back into the bedroom where they have another round of steamy sex. After they take a shower together, Claude suggests they go to the park and celebrate with a picnic. They grabbed a blanket and stopped by Tata's for some light snacks. Once they find a nice comfy spot by the lake, they lay down wrapped in each other's arms. A charming breeze rippled across the lake as a blue herring does a graceful and silent flyby. An agile maple leaf dives from the top of the tree flipping all the way down to join the small waves onto a new journey. While they enjoy the moment, Travaughn is walking by holding hands with his boyfriend. Claude yells out "Hey there – Travaughn, from City Bank! How's it going? I'd like you to meet my love and future wife, Linda!" Travaughn smiled and gave Claude a hug and said, "I'm so happy for you darling, everybody needs love, take care now!" As they continued their walk down the path, Travaughn's boyfriend whispered something in his ear.

Linda rubbed Claude's back and said, "Ok, love, let's get back" He said, "Yes, I can't wait to start writing!" As they head back they see Dave the Ice Cream Man by the basketball courts. "Linda, sweetie, how would you like some ice cream? My treat?" "No way! Too fattening! Gotta stay thin!" she says laughing. They returned to Claude's apartment and for the next month he worked feverishly at creating four short stories. Linda is there every step of the way encouraging him and giving him the love and support he needs.

Knock, knock! "Claude, hey buddy, its Frank can we talk?"

Claude dashed to the door with rent money in hand. "Sorry, Frank can't talk now. Here's the rent, though. Oh! Oh! And try Mann's anti-gas formula, it's the best! See ya, gotta go!" Claude slammed the door and got back to work. A few days later his four short stories are complete. Linda gives him a big, juicy congratulatory kiss and hug. Claude said, "I am so excited! My book goes on the market tomorrow!" She replied "You did it, baby!" Claude holds her and says "No, we did it my love, we did it. I never could have done this without you. You came into my life when I was broken and weak inside, you rekindled my spirit and gave my life meaning again! I love you so much and can't wait for our wedding bells to ring! I'm whole again!" Claude held her tight and put his face in her hair. "Hey babe, love those bright streaks in your hair ... they're hot!" Linda put her hands to Claude's face and gave him a deep and long kiss. She gave him a loving and yearning look and said, "I'm so happy we've been brought together, I'm finally so happy! I'm going to run down to Tata's and get a snack. Do you want anything?" He answered, happily, calmly, "No, babe, just want you to hurry back!" She replied, "Yes, sir" with her gentle smile.

As she headed off to the store, Claude got a call from the publisher. "Hey there, Claude! You did it, you crazy S.O.B! The early reviews are coming back marvelously. Looks like this book of shorts will go to the best seller list. Congratulations!" Claude replied, "Oh thank you, but I owe all my inspiration to my future wife." Hesitating, the publisher said, "Hey man, whatever floats your boat, just keep writing that great shit, we'll be back on top baby, back on top! Ok man, talk to ya tomorrow" Claude murmured, "Um, ok bye!" and scratched his head. He said aloud, "Freaking guy is weird!"

The store Linda went to was only fifteen minutes away but an hour had passed and Linda had not returned. Claude peeked out the window to see if his love was walking back, then his eyes took in the angry black night. A heavy blue rain began and Claude worried. He nervously paced back and forth in the kitchen, stopping by the window at each turn. When anxiety finally overtook him, he grabbed his rain coat and headed for the door.

Just as he was about to walk out Frank was standing there, confronting him. "Claude, my friend, we need to speak!" Claude said, "Sorry, I gotta go, I'm waiting for Linda and..." "Claude please!" "God damn it, Frank! I don't want to date your fucking sister! I'm getting married! Fuck! I gotta go get Linda!!!" Then Frank interrupted with his booming voice. "Claude! There is no Linda Ramos!" Claude went static for a moment, and then went into a hearty laugh. He pointed at Frank as if he had pie in his face. "Ha, ha, you're funny, you're a sick dude you know that, you need help, look it, I have to go. The rain is getting worse!"

"Look, Claude, you have to stop doing this to yourself, it's going to be ok!"

"Enough of this crazy bullshit Frank! Enough! Have you been shooting that shit your sister was on? Huh?" Shaking his head, Frank said, "Claude, please, I'm trying to help.

There are things you need to know!" Stunned, suspicious, Claude said, "What the fuck do I need to know? What Frank? What? I know all I need to know. I found the love of my life and she is Linda Ramos, and she's out there, she's out there!" Claude circled the kitchen like a squirrel looking for an exit.

Frank looked at the floor, took a deep breath, and said, "When you told me about this great girl you met, I wanted to meet her because I never saw her. You told me she lives at 19 Pinecrest Ave. so I went by there to meet her. Claude! That house has been vacant for over six years! The last person who lived at that address was a woman named Rachael Moore."

Claude felt as though his entire insides dropped to his feet and turned into toxic lead. He began shaking and sweating, his speech became pressured and rapid. "W-w-what the fuck are you saying, Frank? What the fuck are you saying? You're nuts, Frank! Nuts! I- I-I picked her up. I've been to her house a dozen times. I was in there, had coffee! Dinner! I took a piss in her bathroom. You're crazy. You're crazy!- Stop fucking with me! "

Claude feverishly looked out the window for Linda, like a sports fan fighting for a better view. "This can't be! Ok, ok Frank, that's enough, I have to go!"

"Claude, there's more to the story. Apparently this Rachael Moore grew up in foster homes and I got in touch with one of her first foster parents who took over the house. She told me when Rachael was buried it was a sad and lonely funeral service. The best thing she could do for Rachael was to put her favorite precious doll that the foster mother saved for her since she was a little girl in her coffin. Claude! When Rachael was little she named the doll. She told me the name was Linda Ramos."

Suddenly Claude let out a heart-stopping scream, and threw a chair out the window "Aaaaarg! Nooooooo! This can't be!"

Frank tried to calm him down, "Now Claude, I don't understand all this either, but..." Claude bolted past Frank, ran downstairs and searched for his love. He scoured the streets of Reedsville in the pouring and unforgiving rain for two hours then went by her house. When he pulled up to the house he is sickened by the sight. He got out of his car and collapsed to his knees and stared in shock. With the rain and wind pounding his face, he looked on at a decrepit, dilapidated grey house. The front door was gone, every window was broken out and it was riddled with graffiti and a trail of empty cigarette packs, soda and beer bottles led inside. Claude slowly pulled himself up and limped in. The walls were bare down to the wood and were beginning to rot. He walked slowly over to a corner in the front room avoiding the musty and stinging water leaking down on him. He looked down to see a frayed, dirty and waterlogged copy of the first book he wrote. Next to it were some syringe needles that were about a year old. He walked back outside to the howling wind and rain and stared at the house for about thirty minutes. Suddenly he cried out, "Lindaaaa! Lindaaaaaaa! Lindaaaa! Where are you? You're real! You're real!" He paced around in circles, splashing mud while holding his hands over his ears. He keeled over and fell to the ground as if kicked in the groin. He wormed around on the ground screaming and crying. He abruptly jumped up and made a crazed dash for his car and took off heading to the cemetery. Soaked and wet, muddy with his hair stuck to his face, he scoured the cemetery looking for Rachael's grave. The darkness was only briefly illuminated by the sudden flash of lightning, exposing the spade shovel he carried over his shoulder. Like a beam of blue fire, the lightning revealed Rachael's grave. Claude fell on his hands in the mud, put his face right next to her name, and screamed out again. "Lindaaaaa!" He started digging like a madman, not stopping till the old coffin was exposed. He rubbed his hands across the coffin as his mind drifted into making love to Linda. Suddenly he snapped back and slapped the mud away. After a few tugs he opened the coffin. There it was: a body decayed to the bones with thin remnants of long red hair still visible on the gruesome skull. Under the brittle vestiges of her left hand was the doll, Linda. Linda Ramos. The long, black, shiny hair that was once on the doll is now also frayed and withered. Claude picked up the doll and cradled it like a baby as he rubbed and caressed it. He put his head down and cried; his tears as heavy as the rain and his pain deeper than the booming thunder. He screamed out again. "Aaaaaarg! Nooooo!" Dirty, torn and tattered, he painfully shuffled back to his apartment. With the doll still cradled in his arms, he sat quietly gazing out the window with a stare as blank as the doll's.

Frank's sister stood in his doorway, tightly holding her one-year sobriety coin.

⌘ ⌘ ⌘

Mattawamp

꩜

In the year 1650, a special and sacred ceremony for the People of the Fresh Water, the *Nipmuc*, was about to take place. It happened at the village of *Wekabaug* which sat near the southern border of an appealing pond and across from the *Quaboag* River. Twenty-five *wetus*, all made from the finest white cedar bark and cattail reeds, stood in a circle overlooking the river and the western hillside. At the center of the communities' homes was their sacred fire and ceremonial long house where council was held by the *sachems*, *pau was*, clan mothers and the people. The pristine, vigorous river was home to life-giving long nose sucker, brook lamprey, fresh water clams, and salmon along with other favorite fresh-water fish of the tribe. Down past the willow tree, some of the men were making ceremonial offerings to the waters. They put tobacco in the *hupuonck*, lit it and said a prayer as they passed it to one another. They gave thanks to all and stepped to the edge of the newly-made fish weir. With their spears ready, they prepared to gather up that day's catch to be smoked for the coming feast.

Dozens of women harvested the sweet summer corn from the field that stretched a mile along the river way. Young girls were nearby filling the beautifully designed, split-ash baskets with blackberries, blueberries, and strawberries to prepare delicious drinks as well as to flavor the roasted meats. Many of the children huddled by the big oak tree on the western side of the village and played *hub bub* or swapped tales of adventure and bravery. Birch, pine, chestnut, and hemlock trees cascaded like a surging green canopy pouring life in every direction. Deer, elk, bear, wolf, beaver, catamount, lynx, moose and many other animals were neighbors. Signs of Creator were everywhere and the sky was abundant with his messenger: the bald and golden eagle.

Manitoo blessed the *Nipmuc* with this land since the beginning of time and put all on Mother Earth for their survival. But more importantly, the *Nipmuc* were to live in harmony with all. Since *Manitoo* put water, trees, four-legged and the winged here first, they are all the teachers. Today, the son of the supreme *pau was* would become a man and be taught these lessons as he goes on his vision journey.

Fourteen year-old *Mattawamp* was a precocious and caring boy. He was tall for his age and had a thin, lean frame. His hair was worn in two long braids that hung down over his brown chest. His eyes were as sharp as a hawk's and balanced by his soft and gentle face. Like his father *Anoosu*, it seems he was born to be a *pau was*. He had been listening to the teachings of the clan mothers, elders and his father since his ears first began to receive the words. While most of the young boys would be out playing *hub bub,* stick games, or catching turtles down by the river, he would stay behind and sit in the back of the longhouse and listen to the elders and *sachems* for hours. However, he would find time for his best friend *Wequash.* She was the beautiful daughter of the *sachem* and was a year younger than him. She was petite with light brown skin; her eyes were golden brown, and she had a laugh that captured *Mattawamp's* heart. Although they were both young and just friends, the elders felt they would be a perfect match for the future. She would work on weaving and shaping her corn husk dolls while she waited for him to come out of the longhouse. Fresh berries and *yokeg* would be a treat she prepared for him; in return, he would take her out canoeing. They loved to flow across the beautiful *Quaboag*. Next to eating smoked eel, this was the most favorite part of their day. They splashed and laughed down the vibrant river as they waved to beavers and leaping fish while a flock of ducks opened a path. After an exuberating voyage they would take a break by the hefty birch tree and sit on the huge rock along the river. After they had a snack, *Wequash* would ask about what was said in the longhouse. But most of all, she enjoyed hearing about *Mattawamp's* dreams. Nobody in the village spoke English but the translation would have been: "*Mattawamp,* what dreams did you have last night?" she asked with a kind smile. The sound of the bubbling waters added tranquil reflection to the question. He sent her a little beam of thankfulness for the question as he tossed a stone in the flowing waters. "Not of you, of course, ha ha." Gently, she tugged one of his braids. "Just kidding – just kidding, but you know what? I dreamt I was a salmon with long braids and all the other fish wanted them because they were the longest. One of them attacked me and clawed my chest so I left the water and hid in the corn fields. But then when I looked at the corn it was an ugly site. All the corn was covered with red spots and the crow was telling me not to eat it. Then I saw my father and the other *pau was*; they were trying to do Green Corn Moon Ceremony but there was something wrong. I didn't see tobacco or sweet grass. They were holding strange objects; they looked like two hard rods made of stone that crossed each other but I don't think it was stone. I don't understand it, *Wequash!*" *Wequash* replied, "Well, that's some dream, *Mattawamp,* but I don't know what it means either ... maybe it means you're gonna make me smoked salmon and corn -ha ha." As she laughed, she tugged his braids again and ran through the woods. *Mattawamp* grinned and said, "Ok, I'm gonna get you for that!" He gives chase past the raspberry bushes.

Everybody in the village as well as neighboring *Nipmuc* clans loved *Mattawamp* – all except one seventeen year-old boy of their tribe named *Kous.* The two boys have known each other since birth but never became close friends because *Kous* was a spiteful and troubled child that would try to get *Mattawamp* in trouble.

When *Mattawamp* was just ten, one of the clan mothers said she had a vision that he would be a great healer of the people and an honor song was sung for the young prodigy. That same evening when *Mattawamp* was down at the lake swimming with the other boys and girls, *Kous* came up from behind and pulled him under the water. As *Mattawamp* was thrashing under the water for air, *Kous* was laughing. "Ha, ha, the old witch is wrong! Some leader you are! Ha, ha" *Wequash* screamed out, "Get off him, you toad!" *Kous* dunked him five times before some of the clan mothers came and scolded him. "*Kous* stop it now! When will you learn, boy? You're always in trouble! Just for that, you will go and harvest corn tomorrow; you need to learn the balance and unity of all things!" All the other kids laughed at *Kous* because he would now miss out on all the games they had planned for the day. *Kous* scowled at the other children and said, "Don't laugh you little dogs; I'll get you all, you'll see, you stinking dogs!" Then there was the time *Kous* stole *Mattawamp's* moccasins that his grandmother made for him. He painted them with red ochre to hide the family symbol of the crow. He would have gotten away with it except he forgot the bottom which displayed a huge crow painted in blueberry dye. Once the elders found out, nobody saw him for a week. *Kous* could never seem to stay out of trouble or stop finding ways to harass *Mattawamp.*

Even on this special day, *Kous* was there to offer his words of encouragement. "You're not going to make it you know! Five days on your own, deep in the forest in some strange land! They say there are creatures with giant pointy teeth made from rock, they eat little boys, they come out of the mountains and grind you up. Then they piss on you and drink you like mush! You're a fool, *Mattawamp,* if you go, that's why I never go!" *Kous* failed to tell the truth, which was that the Elders have not permitted him to go. *Mattawamp* looked up to the sky and saw a bald eagle circling overhead. He turned to *Kous* with a smile, "Well, if I'm to be grinded and pissed on, than I shall return to mother earth and come back as a huge pine tree, tall and smelling clean!" *Kous* stared angrily and said, "Well, I'm telling you, it will be painful and horrible, you will suffer greatly. Don't be a fool!" *Mattawamp* replied "*Kous,* the elders have taught me that life is not about good or bad things happening to us, they are all just experiences for us to learn from. If I must feel pain to grow then I am prepared for that. Nothing worthwhile will come easily." *Kous* pushed *Mattawamp* in the chest and said, "Ah, shut up with all that longhouse talk it's so boring, so boring!" *Kous* smacks him in the back as he walks away and said, "well, have fun, little dog, ha ha!"

Mattawamp was accustomed to his foul behavior and actually felt sorry for *Kous,* fearing he would never change. Despite the nonsense, he was ready to take the journey and returned to his lodge to prepare his spirit. Even though today brought him closer to his passion of being a great medicine man like his father *Anoosu,* he still needed to complete his vision journey. Back at the longhouse there was the sound of the water drum beating to the rhythm of Mother Earth. Soon the drumming was joined by the chanting of several voices and their calls: *Mattawamp! Mattawamp!*

Mattawamp's mother smiled with tears in her eyes as she gave her son a small bundle of tobacco wrapped in a corn leaf. Following a big hug, she escorted him out of the *wetu* and to the sacred fire. The soft-spoken boy was nervous but also anxious to begin his journey. He took a deep breath, threw his two long braids toward his back, held his head high and walked forward to his destiny.

As he walked toward the longhouse he saw that all the people had made a circle around the sacred fire. *Wequash* stood there with a big smile; her buckskin dress had the emblems of strawberries and vines going down the side while her hair was braided back and enlaced with little, pretty shells. From clan mothers to chiefs, warriors to children, they were all there dressed in their finest buckskin to send prayers for their future *Pau Was*. *Kous* was there, too, but had to be forced by his mother twice – once to actually go, and second to wear something proper instead of his filthy hides he wears to clean and gut fish. *Mattawamp* was escorted to the center and *Anoosu* was there to greet him with a proud but serious smile. The yellow and white paint on his father's face stopped when it joined with the head band of purple and white wampum. Symbols of the crow, moon and patterns of stars matching the night sky were designed in the small shell beads. They were attached by thirteen eagle feathers that stood straight up around his head. His ears were interlaced with strips of copper with lines and curls etched in them. These designs signified their clan and were also on his copper arm bands. Around his neck were large bear claws which represent the spirit of healing and protecting medicine. Also, an eagle bone whistle was worn to communicate with the Land of Endless Spirits and a porcupine quill leather pouch holding sacred herbs was hung from his neck. Standing close by to honor the event was *Wequash's* father, the *sachem*. His deer antler headdress was also complimented with elegant wampum. He also sported his beautiful cape over his shoulders made from turkey feathers that *Wequash* and her mother made during the winter. Next to the sacred fire, was a red clay bowl with a mixture of tobacco, cedar and sweet grass. *Anoosu* took a small twig from the ground, put one end in the sacred fire, and used it to light the ceremonial mixture. Once lit, he waved the smoke with an eagle feather gently around the circle as he recited a prayer. As he moved about the circle, his chant was accompanied by the sound of his turtle shell rattle as he passed it close to the earth, sky and to the four directions. The cleansing smoke spiraled around as it carried up all the prayers to *Manitoo*. Then he fanned the smoke all around *Mattawamp* and repeated another prayer as another song on the water drum began.

At the end of the song, *Anoosu* turned to his son. "*Mattawamp,* my dear son; since your birth we all knew it was a special day, for you were born under the Sky of Power. A great thunder storm and shaking of Mother Earth brought you to this world. The elders have seen your medicine in dreams and yet you remain a humble and honest child. So this is why today, my son, you shall take your own vision journey. Feel Mother Earth, look into the spirit of the animals and communicate with the stars and the night sky. Let Father Sun brighten your knowledge of all these things. May the Land of Endless Spirits where our ancestors dwell share with you the medicine and stories of the sky beings." While *Anoosu* continued with his guiding words for his son, he was rudely interrupted by a loud and vulgar burp. The people all turned to *Kous*, some looking angrily and others shaking their heads. *Kous* just shrugged his shoulders as he smiled like a cat that had just swallowed a mouse. At that moment,

Kous's mother gave him a swift kick in the buckskin and the ceremony continued. *Anoosu* looked at *Kous* sharply and cleared his throat and turned back to his son. "Ok, my son, it is time. You are about to embark on a sacred and mysterious journey. But also it may be dangerous, and as your father I worry, but as the *Pau Was* of our clan, I know whatever *Manitoo* chooses for your path will be the way it was meant to be. The clan mother's vision is strong, but if you are called to the Land of Endless Sprits than I shall see you when my body is done and I return to the sky to greet you." *Anoosu* gave his son a long hug then handed him a bundle of sacred herbs and the turtle shell rattle. *Mattawamp's* mother also grabbed her son tightly one last time before he left to either die, or to become a man.

Elders and other tribal members came up and offered words of support as two warriors walked up to *Mattawamp* and prepared him for his journey. *Sepham,* who is one of the greatest hunters in the village, handed him a ten-inch knife that he carved from moose bone and antler. The top part of *Sepham's* chest is painted black. His forehead is painted red and one side of his face has three black lines. On one shoulder he had a tattoo of a bear paw and on the other an image of a wolf.

Next, the brave and strong *Pemsqouh* walked over with a leather strip and blindfolded *Mattawamp*. *Pemsquoh's* hair was completely shaven except for top of his head. The front part was shined with bear grease and combed over the side of his head. The back was separated by hawk and turkey feathers and made into scissor tail braids that went half down his back. His face had red zig zag lines that started at his chin and went to his hairline. His legs had similar markings that went from his ankles to his knees. Both men had a full quiver of arrows and an ax lashed around their waists. With a look of concern but joy, *Anoosu* watched as his son was lead out of the village. The two warriors led him north on a two-day trek beyond the Great Winding River. They speak only briefly to *Mattawamp* as they guide him through thick forests, swamps and over the hills. At one point, *Mattawamp* was put into a canoe. Still blindfolded, he could only guess where he was going. Briefly he had an image of giant monsters with large stone teeth with blood dripping off them. After a few more hours they reached their destination. *Pemsqouh* removed the blindfold and said, "*Mattawamp,* I have watched you since you were brought into the world and now your time has come. Follow your heart, listen to Sprits and let the forest teach you the old ways."

Sepham nodded his head as he put his arm on his shoulder and said, "You will do well. For five Suns, you shall stay in this place alone and find your vision; you shall fast for the first four, and then on the fifth you may find your own meal. After that, you must ask the Spirits to guide you home. Remember the teachings and lessons of the Long House. Be well!" At that moment the two warriors fade away into the woods. *Mattawamp* is all alone. He is in a far off place on the border of their longtime rivals, the *Haudenosaunee.* However, he was not afraid but more concerned that the animals of these woods did not know him. He was there to learn from them and gain understanding of the Sky Beings. As he looked north he noticed the high gray and blue mountains climbing into the Sun. Then he looked west in the direction where the Sky Beings travel and felt a powerful chill that the Ancestors were with him.

While he inhaled the beauty around him he turned south as his soul traversed down the Great Winding River like an artery connecting to the heart of the Earth. As he gazed east, he reflected on his purpose: this was the Land of the Fresh Water, his home and the people he wished to serve. His destiny to be *Pau Was* was at hand. The warriors chose a flat spot on the edge of a small hill. *Mattawamp* began gathering stones about the size of small pumpkins. He then put them in a complete circle and sprinkled tobacco along the edges. In addition he went to a nearby cedar tree and got some of the flat branches and placed them in the circle. Next he walked one time around the circle then stepped inside and sat down. As the Sun began to set, *Mattawamp* began to meditate and settle in. But when the indigo Moon took over the night, the increasingly loud chatter of the woods gave him trouble relaxing. He couldn't help flinching from time to time as the cacophony of shrieks and calls bellowed in the unfamiliar darkness.

The bright moon created odd shadows and figures that seemed to be lurking all around him. Just as fear began to overtake him, he remembered some of the old songs from the longhouse. He took out the turtle rattle and began to sing. "Yah-dah-hah-yah dah; yah-hey-yo!" His mind became more relaxed as he sang through the night. At first light he stepped out of the circle with a growling stomach. *Mattawamp* pondered his mother's smoked eel and corn cake, with perhaps some fresh blueberries on top, but he knew this longing for food was just the beginning of his tests. Most of the day was spent looking around his area. He took notice of every living thing he saw. He watched a caterpillar climb an oak tree. After that he spent some time trailing a porcupine; followed by quietly observing a family of raccoons. The furry masked critters made a sudden escape up a chestnut tree as a stunningly fast pack of wolves darted through the woodland glade. From time to time a big crow would come and check in on him and let out a big "caw-caw!" just to let him know he was there. *Mattawamp* would look into the eyes of the crow and smile, seeing him put his mind at greater ease. "Thank you, brother," he yelled up. After some more scouting and ignoring his belly, he went back in the circle.

Just as he was about to sit he was startled by a gigantic catamount. The big cat darted passed him in hot pursuit of a young deer. Nothing but a brief dust up of leaves and undergrowth as both animals disappeared into the brush. As night came, it brought an immense thunder storm with it. The clouds rolled in with force followed by a gushing rain. Wind soon came to join the party bringing a cold chill to the dark. *Mattawamp* sat intrepidly with the pouring rain bouncing off his shivering body. He took out the rattle to sing to keep his thoughts off his cold, wet, and hungry body. But just as he began, booming and crashing thunder wanted to be heard first. Lightning was striking all around. He thought for a moment his life was in jeopardy but then had a revelation. The words of his father came though on a flash of lightning. This was the "Sky of Power!" At that moment he knew something was happening, the Sprits were coming! He bravely stood up as the rain and wind crashed against him. He held the rattle to the sky and shouted, "Thank you my relatives! I am here! I am here! Show me the way! Show me the way!" Thunder and lightning became so intense that night was like day as the wind howled like a pack of hungry wolves. In the midst of the mighty storm, *Mattawamp* chanted the old songs for four hours. Then in an instant, as he was waving the rattle to the sky, a glowing flash made contact and *Mattawamp* collapsed. While his body lay in the circle, his spirit floated past the storm up to the stars. He was in awe as he watched the flashing and swirling clouds from above. Then he moved on to circle the moon. When he looked down to Mother Earth he saw his beautiful village. With a leaping swan dive he propelled himself straight to *Wekabaug*, cutting through the air like a charging hawk, but he landed with the grace of a dove. He heard the sound of the water drum coming from the longhouse and he walked in. Inside he sees all the people laughing, dancing, and eating. He saw fresh fiddle heads, corn, smoked eel, roasted deer, and berries displayed in finely carved wooden bowls. The people were in a long line dancing and shaking rattles. It was a beautiful sight! *Mattawamp* began singing and joined in the line. As he came around the circle, his eyes were captured by the food. He reached over to get just a little taste of that smoked eel. Just as he tried to grab it, he was yanked away by something and pulled out of the longhouse. When he turned around there stood the mighty Thunderbird. *Mattawamp* fell to his knees in awe. Its eyes were as sharp as the sun and each wing was bigger than the entire longhouse. It gave *Mattawamp* a serious look. *Mattawamp* was shaken by the moment and said, "Ah – ah I know, I am fasting, but-but!" Thunderbird did not speak but talked to him with his mind. That is when *Mattawamp* realized Thunderbird was not upset with him for trying to eat but for some reason did not want him at his village. Thunderbird's look was not stern but more of a compassionate gaze.

Thunderbird looked *Mattawamp* up and down, then grabbed him and shot him back into the sky. This time *Mattawamp* was beyond the moon and the stars of the night. He was taken to a celestial, majestic village where each *wetu* and longhouse was constructed from glowing blue stars. Thunderbird conveyed to *Mattawamp* that he must visit each lodge and then the longhouse. Done with his instructions, the fiery red bird suddenly blasted away into the distant stars. *Mattawamp* went into the first lodge and found that it was the house of Spider. There, through many stories told by the elders of the spider's camp, he learned the mystery, importance and power of the little unseen things as well as the significance of keeping all life in balance. Then he was in the house of the Bear. Protecting and defending the medicine, as well as being brave, were the teachings in his lodge. Next, he was in the place of Deer and the lessons of peace, love, and compassion were instilled in him. Loyalty, respect, and defending the family were the guidance in the *wetu* of Wolves. Then, on to the house of the Crow. Magic, mystery and the ability to communicate in the dream world, along with the gift to adapt to any environment, were taught in this lodge. The enigmatic oceans and rivers were revealed in the lodge of the Salmon. Down the line of *wetu's* he went. Ant, Beaver, Crane and so on.

Finally, he reached the longhouse made from the breath of the universe. When he walked in, it was as though he had entered another realm. Above him, there were unfamiliar and bizarre planets circling two Suns, one red and the other blue. Below him was a gushing neon-purple river. Off in the distance of the lilac waters he noticed a little dot. As the dot became closer it revealed itself to be the most beautiful birch bark canoe he'd ever seen. It was strong with gorgeous designs on the side with the carving of Thunderbird in front. Inside the canoe was the Sky Beings and they were bringing *Mattawamp* the Sacred Basket containing the final knowledge for him to become *Pau Was*. They paddled closer and closer; *Mattawamp* did his best to appear patient but his heart yearned for this moment. As they gracefully rowed next to him, one Sky Being smiled and held up the basket to him. The basket was glowing like the sun and had sparkles of small stars of many colors dancing around it. *Mattawamp* cautiously reached out to take it and smiled back at the Sky Being. *Mattawamp* bowed his head to receive the precious gift and closed his eyes for a moment. When he re-opens them, he looks down and the basket has turned into an ax covered in blood. Simultaneously, the Sky Being shouted one word to *Mattawamp:* "FIGHT!"

Like a shooting star, *Mattawamp's* spirit is propelled back to his circle in the woods. He awakens groggy, shaken and a bit confused. Five days have passed while he was on this Vision Journey which completed his quest. His thirst and hunger were overtaken by the power of his experience. Although he felt blessed and rejuvenated, he still had more questions than answers. The command "fight" from the Sky Being was not what he expected, plus he was not sure whether he really saw a basket or a bloody ax. What further troubled him was the big owl sitting in the spot where the crow was. He did his best to put those thoughts behind him and focused on the fact he completed his vision journey. He said a prayer, thanking *Manitoo* for the journey, and headed down to the stream for a drink and a meal. After taking a long drink, he caught a few fish and roasted them over a small fire. While munching on his catch, he was filled with much excitement. He couldn't wait to tell his mother and father of his grand adventure but he also wanted to see *Wequash.* He went back to dismantle his circle and return the stones to their original places when he noticed some fine dark blue grapes growing nearby.

He went to gather up a bunch to take back to *Wequash* and enjoyed a generous sample while he worked. He savored the sweet taste and thought how pleased she would be because they did not grow quite so tastily back home. Right in that moment, fifteen Mohawk warriors painted and dressed for battle appeared from behind the thicket. *Mattawamp* took a defensive stance as the men surrounded him. The leader of the group, named *Tso Ka'We,* rushed over and removed his knife from his sheath and put it to *Mattawamp's* throat. With an angry face the man said, "Do you know where you are ... boy?" Mattawamp looked at him just as angrily and said "I am not a boy! I am a Man!"

Tso Ka'We looked around at the others and then back at *Mattawamp* and said, "Well is this... *man,* from *Susquehannock* or *Sokoki?* I've lost many arrows inside the hearts of you dogs." *Mattawamp* held his position and replied, "No!

I am *Mattawamp*! I am *Nipmuc* from *Wekabaug,* clan of the Crow, son of *Anoosu* and next *PauWas*! I do not fear your blade or your arrows. I have dwelt in the land of the Sky Beings and walked below the Earth. I flew with Thunderbird and touched the stars in the Lodge of Mystery and Wisdom. The Moon will shake blinding dust in your eyes and burn your flesh while the Sun dissolves your hearts like the morning mist. Your silly weapons have no power over me, for I was born under the Sky of Power. So take this body if you wish and I shall return to the Land of Endless Sprits. And if *Manitoo* wishes, I will show you mercy and not haunt your dreams for a thousand winters." A few of the Mohawks looked nervously at each other while *Tso Ka'We* took the blade from his throat. His angry grimace changed to a smile, then he burst into a hearty laugh.

As the laughter slowed, *Tso Ka'We* patted Mattawamp on the back and said, "*Pau was.* That is good-that is good. With the malignant illness upon our people, we need more Hand Tremblers like you. But I must tell you what I saw when I looked into your eyes, I saw a warrior ready to kill." *Mattawamp* replied, "Well, I never had a knife to my neck before, so ..." *Mattawamp* was distracted from his thought when he noticed one of the Mohawks with a string of beaver pelts over his shoulder. *Mattawamp* asked him, 'Why have you killed so many? What can you get from all their deaths?" The Mohawk responded with, "I did not kill them. It was a band of Dutch. They killed the beaver and we killed them." *Mattawamp* looked puzzled. "Dutch? What clan are they from?"

"They are from the 'Coat Men' with the unfinished skin and hair on their faces, like the ass of a dog. I'm not sure if they're human beings or not. They're like a creature with an endless appetite: the more it gets, the more it wants. They hunt and kill everything they see, then trade it for the stones of the Earth. And what's more, they have a malevolent drink that controls your thoughts. Once you drink it, you are bewitched and can no longer refuse it! My own uncle was enchanted by this poison and jumped from the Great Falls!" *Mattawamp* shook his head and said, "Yes-yes, I think I remember talk of these people in the longhouse. It was said to stay away from them, that they're crazy and practice strange sorcery to steal our souls." *Tso Ka'We* interrupted and said, "Pray you never see them, *PauWas*. Pray! You're people and mine have had many great battles through the years. We fought *Nipmuc* since the days my grandfathers were but children. But today I don't call you my enemy. There's a great sickness that surrounds all the human beings of our clans. I think it's caused by the gluttony of the 'Coat Men' and will spread like a shadow before the setting sun. Travel in peace, *Mattawamp*; safe journey back to the land of *Wekabaug*." All the Mohawks began walking away and as they did, each one touched *Mattawamp* on the shoulder. When *Tso Ka'We* was about to walk away, *Mattawamp* gave him the moose carved knife. "This is for you, *Tso Ka'We*. It is made by one of our warriors; I am a healer, not a killer." *Tso Ka'We* took the knife and held it to his chest as he dipped his head slightly in appreciation. And in an instant, the Mohawks vanished into the woods.

Coupled with the words of the Mohawks and his vision, *Mattawamp* was troubled. But all he could think about was getting back to *Wekabaug* to show all the people that he had survived, and returned with a vision. He headed back towards the Winding River so that it would guide him home. Cutting through small trails and making new ones, several hours later he was at the shores of the rushing waters. Not far off he saw a band of *Pocumtuc's*. The men were fishing and a few of them were working on a net made from hemp. The children played and were catching small frogs and bugs by the shore. Two of the beautiful women's faces were hidden by their long black flowing hair as they leaned over the bowl and pestle pounding corn. Four other young men were sitting under the willow tree carving spoons and bowls from ash burl as they shared jokes. *Mattawamp* yelled out to the men fishing "Hey!" As he walked towards the encampment. The people all smiled and greeted him, then one man jokingly said, "Hey *Nipmuc,* you're on the wrong side of the river, ha, ha!" *Mattawamp* laughed and said, "How are you, my brothers and sisters, it does my heart good to see you! I'm on my way to *Wekabaug,* returning from a vision journey, and I have many stories to share." Once he said that, all the people came around him and gave him hugs and pats on the head. A lovely eighteen year-old girl walked up to him with a perfect basket made from the bark of basswood and decorated with porcupine quills and stiff guard hair from a moose. The beautiful basket was full of berries and *yokeg.* She gave him an animated smile and said, "Eat! You must by hungry!" He humbly replied, "Thank You!" As he chomped down all the treats. Next, an Elder of the *Pocumtuc* stood over *Mattawamp* and gave a blessing. Then a few other men let out a loud "whoop –whoop!" Then one of them held two carved sticks. He began tapping them together and singing and dancing. Soon after, others joined in behind him shaking their gourd rattles. The man holding the sticks called out a chant and all the others responded by repeating his words as their feet stomped and they danced to the beat of the sticks. *Mattawamp* joined in the dance as they formed a snake-like line up and down the peaceful shore. Finally, the procession turned into a circle and in unity they all ran to the center laughing and whooping. *Mattawamp* wiped the sweat from his forehead and sat on a log and watched as another round of dancing began. The dancing and eating reminded him of his beautiful *Wequash* and how much he wanted to get home to his family. "Thank you all so much but I must be going now."

One of the men said to *Mattawamp.* "I have a fine canoe to take you across the river, my young brother!" *Mattawamp* smiled at him and said, "Ah, thank you, but I think the elders didn't want me to cross that way; to complete my journey I must make it on my own." The man nods his head and says "Yes, of course, but be careful, the river can be rough as a bear's growl." They all said their farewells as *Mattawamp* headed down the shoreline looking for the best spot to cross. He found a point a few miles down that was not too bad; it was a little over a half mile across and the waters seemed calm. Above him he heard a loud "Caw! Click, Click-Caw-Caw!" It was Crow sitting at the edge of a sycamore branch. *Mattawamp* looked up with a smile and said, "What is it brother? Should I have taken the canoe?" He said with a laugh, "Don't worry, I can do this!"

He took a hard look at a floating branch speeding by, and reflected on how much bigger the river was than the one back home. Then with an aggressive leap, he began to swim. He breathed deeply, in and out, as his skinny legs and arms battled the current. The strong river current began to pick up velocity as the mounting waves smacked his face. His body disappeared; then reappeared as he bobbed up and down between the white wrinkles. Just as he reached the middle point of the river, the power of the flow overtook him.

He stroked with all his might, but he does not make any progress. His hard work was barely enough to keep him afloat! Then suddenly a ten foot sturgeon swam rapidly up from underneath towards him. It mistakes one of his dangling, long braids for a tasty snack and grabbed onto it. The goliath fish dragged *Mattawamp* by his hair fifty feet down to the bottom of the river! Two minutes elapsed as *Mattawamp* struggled to pull his hair out from the sturgeon's mouth who now sat as static as a bolder holding its prize. He tugged and twisted but the fish is too big and too strong. His body began to go weak as he struggled to hold his breath. Air bubbles began to come out of his mouth while his spirit drifted toward the sky. At the same moment that his lungs surrender to the water, though, a colossal snapping turtle, as big as the sturgeon, decided that she wanted the treat, too. She lunged in and bit the hair free. The massive, shelled giant tasted the hair and quickly spit it back out. With a powerful fluttering burst, she swam for the surface and *Mattawamp* grabbed onto her back with his last bit of strength.

As the turtle hovered effortlessly over the river, *Mattawamp* rested on her back and coughed up water. She allowed him to stay until he was about fifteen feet from shore. With a swift buck, she launches him off her back and she then headed back for the deep water. *Mattawamp* scrambled to shore and collapsed with his cheek to the sand. The crow swooped by and gave out one loud "caw" as it took off through the trees. With his head still on the ground, *Mattawamp* said with a moan and cough "Uuh … ooh … yes … I know … I should have taken the canoe." He rolled himself over and sat on his rear to rest a bit more. Not far off, there was a family of huge black bear knee-deep in the river snatching up the crimson salmon with their claws. As the sun went down, *Mattawamp* moved in from the coastline and set up camp for the night. He gathered up some pine needles and soft ferns to make a comfortable bed for himself on the south-facing slope.

Mattawamp marveled at the radiant stars that glittered in the night sky as he reflected on his mother's cooking and the stories he will share with the tribe. The howling wolves beyond the ridge don't keep him from falling into a much needed sleep. About an hour before sunrise he began to toss and turn in his sleep. He dreamt that he was back at *Wekabaug* and that there was a big celebration honoring his journey. The people were laughing and dancing and giving him hugs when *Wequash* walked up with a basket of fresh berries. She smiled and made the offer. He smiled back and reached in to take a handful. When he took his hand out, though, it was covered in blood and human entrails. In that moment he awoke abruptly, sweating and breathing heavily. He was so distraught that even though the sun was not quite up, he took off for *Wekabaug* as fast as his legs could carry him.

He cut through swamps and trails like an agile deer. Abruptly his nose and mouth were overtaken by rancid and stinging smoke. Soon after he sees' large amounts of black smoke rising from the direction of his village, he runs faster! Once he reaches home, what he saw there caused his eyes to open wide as he gasped in shock. He fell to his knees in horror. The entire village, his home, his sacred community, was burned to ashes. He began to scream out for his mother and father as he ran to the remains of their home. Between the charred frame of the *wetu* were remnants of his father's headdress. The two remaining eagle feathers that survived were mangled, scalded and broken. The wampum beads were stripped from the singed leather lying by the smashed pottery. He screamed out again at the top of his lungs as he ran to the longhouse that was also scorched to the ground. He saw broken rattles, baskets and other sacred belongings scattered like fallen leaves by the wind. He looked down by the river and saw that the corn fields were hacked to shreds. No food for the people! There was not a soul at the village. He ran from one blistered lodge to the next. He screamed for *Wequash* and his grandparents as he ran around in a state of utter confusion. He wobbled over to the sacred fire that had been smothered with piles of debris. There was an Englishmen's hat blowing in the weeping wind like a foul omen sent from below. *Mattawamp's* heart was as broken and brittle as the village around him. He pulled his hair, looked up and screamed, then *dropped* to the ground with his head to the earth, and cried. And just as he picked up his head, he was met with a musket smashed into his face and he was knocked unconscious.

When he came to, he was united with his family, but they were all locked inside a large human cage waiting to be logged and processed like cattle. They were twenty miles east of their own village, in the newly established "Praying Town." There had been an aggressive and zealous movement under-way by White settlers to relocate and Christianize all *Nipmuc* people per order of the Massachusetts General Court. "Praying Towns," or prisons, were popping up across *Nipmuc* country like a malevolent virus breeding abject sorrow. Village by village, *Nipmucs* and other tribes were dragged from their homes under threat of death, then shackled around the neck and feet. They were corralled and marched into "Praying Towns" at the will of the new settlers who just a few decades before depended on the tribal people to survive. For some, namely the *Nipmuc* warriors, slave traders from the East India Shipping Company intervened with their march. The men would be dragged off to Boston harbor and sold into slavery in the West Indies never to see their family or home again. Once there, they would be worked to death if sorrow or disease didn't free them first. Tribal communities that stood thousands of years, communities that even sur-vived ice ages and other cataclysmic events, were crushed in a blink of an eye by the colonists' ghettoes. And this time it was the beautiful village of *Wekabaug* to be forsaken. *Mattawamp* looked around at the dismal fort through the iron bars as his mother and father hugged him tight. The place was surrounded by a twenty foot stockade and was well-guarded by soldiers and militiamen. He saw three horse-and-wagons which were all packed to the brim with beaver and wolf hides. Also, he saw more wagons that were heading out – those were full of wooden barrels with the markings

"Rum" on them. In addition, he saw Indians but they didn't look like Indians. They were dressed like the English: their hair was short and they had a heavy walk about them but were thin as reeds. They were coming and going from shanties and poorly built homes that they were forced to live in.

The sadness on *Mattawamp's* fathers face was hidden underneath the bruises and blood dried to his flesh. His mother's hair was frayed and dirty and her arms were scraped and bruised. Lined up next to their cell were thirteen other coops with their entire tribe crammed into them. *Mattawamp* ran from one side to the other trying to get a better view into the other cells.

He was looking for *Wequash* but instead saw *Kous* and his father on the far distant side. Both of them were speaking to a Mohegan who was dressed as the English and who stood outside the cage. He couldn't hear the words but they seemed to be pleading with the Mohegan about something. Then from behind him a soft touch pressed his shoulder. It was *Wequash*. She was in the same pen with him along with her parents. They all hugged and moved to the back. Then *Wequash's* father told them to stay strong. Off in the distance the same Mohegan man was standing with several Englishmen who were chatting and holding papers. The Mohegan was named *Sequnu;* he was brought here years ago and served as trusty and translator. One of the Englishmen is the Reverend John Elliot who is the head minister in charge of Christianizing all the Indians.

Also, there was the tough and brutal Captain Thomas Pierce. He despised Indians and everything about them. He was in charge of the subjugation and punishment of all the natives of the "Praying Town." In addition, there was the land speculator Fredrick Whitmore who is eager to usurp Indian lands and sell them for huge profits as well as Daniel Gookin, interested in doing the same. Also amongst them was Matthew Dandy. He was a notorious slave trader and bandit sent to the colonies as punishment for crimes in England. In addition, there was Nathanial Curtis. He was a rugged frontiersmen and trapper who was brought in to help ease relations. He has traded with the Pennacook tribe for years and considered himself a friend to the natives. Nathanial was a short, stocky man with a small beard and wore a leather fringed overcoat with an otter bandoleer. He can speak the native tongue and sometimes he was criticized by the English for dressing more like and Indian than his own kind.

The group of men walked back to where the *Nipmucs* were held captive. As *Sequnu* opened the cages, they were ordered under gun point to line up. They were pushed and shoved into a long line as one Englishmen took a headcount. Captain Pierce smugly walked up and down the column as most of the *Nipmucs* shook and cried. When he came across *Sepham, Pemsqouh* and the other *Nipmuc* warriors, it was a different story.

Pemsqouh hurled a look at the captain that could burn lead and said, "You coward! Why don't you put down the thunder stick and fight me like a man! I don't wish to know your god! Let us go now or I will kill you!" The captain did not understand what *Pemsqouh* said but knew from the tone it was not pleasant. The captain gave him a mean grin then ripped the feathers from his head and stepped on them. As *Pemsqouh* lunged for the captain, he was clubbed to the ground. Shackles were thrown on him and the captain yelled out, "Mr. Dandy, I judge I have a savage fit for haggle. He is a lively sort which shall do well at auction lest his head serve as an alternate trophy. Take him away!" *Pemsqouh* yelled as he was dragged away by three of Mr. Dandy's men. Mr. Dandy yelled to the men. "Be of good cheer lads, we'll have more cargo before the day's end!" Before *Sepham* and others could take any action, muskets and swords were in their faces.

Captain Pierce took a step back to get a good view of the *Nipmucs* and called for *Sequnu.* "*Sequnu,*" he said with a commanding voice. "Relay this message to your people!" *Sequnu* had a look of concern and said, "But my English father, they are not my people, they are of..." *Sequnu* stopped speaking due to the harsh stare from Captain Pierce. That was when Nathaniel Curtis stepped in. "They are *Nipmuc*-sir. Although they speak a similar tongue and share traditions, yet still they are a different society than Mohegan." The Captain turned an arrogant glance toward Curtis and said, "Mind your place Curtis. I have scant need of your correction! You may consider these lowly devils diverse. I, on the other hand, see a multitude of heathen of an equal depraved nature. *Sequnu!* Carry On!" *Sequnu* nodded his head and said, "Yes-yes Captain!"

Captain Pierce paced up and down the row of *Nipmucs* as *Sequnu* interpreted his words. "Today... starts your passage from barbarism to civility... and if your wretched souls are not so beguiled with malignant witchcraft, then the good labor of Minister Elliot should not be in vain. I am Captain Pierce and you are hereby assigned to His Majesty's Praying Town per order of the General Court of Massachusetts. You may not leave this fort, and any attempt to do so will be met with a wholesome lesson. Lieftenant!" When the captain called on the soldier he walked away with two others behind the meeting house. They returned momentarily with a decayed, severed Indian head on a pole and stuck it in the ground in front of the *Nipmucs.* Many of them shrieked and gasped at the repulsive sight. Numerous parents covered the eyes of the children as the women cried. The English soldiers laughed in affirmation to each other while the *Nipmucs* whence at the decapitated native.

The Captain resumed his invectives as *Mattawamp* stood with a numb stare. "Now, then, I see I have your full attention. If you fully obey and learn the ways of the gospel and sever your league with demons, than you shan't meet this ghastly end. Here are but some of the laws and they are subject to change at his majesty's pleasure. You must obey Minister Elliott and take heed to all his lessons. You will learn the gospel and earnestly follow the lesson of our savoir Christ. No dancing, drumming, unlawful visiting, disobeying the Sabbath ,worshipping the sun, trees or any other foolish idles you vile creatures conjure. Further, let it be known, you shall not clothe yourselves with articles from the beasts in the forests. You will immediately cut your hair and wear the proper English clothes and be expected to do your share of daily work! And most of all, under any circumstance, you are not to be in possession of any form of weapon! Disobey any of these laws and you will be beaten and hung from the ramparts!"

Sepham laughed at the words of the Captain and said, "Mohegan, save your translation, his words mean nothing to me. He is a babbling fool that smells like the fart of a sick moose!" *Sequnu* strained to hold back his laugh when the Captain burst in. "What was that the savage said, Sequnu!?' Nathaniel Curtis, who understood the words clearly, also covered his smile and walked away. *Sequnu* said, "Uuh, sir, he said, he thought he smelled roasted moose." Captain Pierce gave *Sequnu* a shifty look as *Sepham* and the other warriors chuckled. Suddenly, Captain Pierce and Mr. Dandy walked away and whispered back and forth. At one point it seemed they were arguing but then they shook hands and Mr. Dandy said, "Fine then, we have an accord!" They walked back over to the row and Captain Pierce said, "You there, the one for the taste for moose; you shall go with Mr. Dandy. Also you, you and you! " The Captain went on to point out forty of the strongest warriors who were then shackled from feet to neck and prepared for slavery. *Sepham* and many others yelled and thrashed around as they were smashed in the head with clubs and muskets. The *sachem* of the tribe leapt forward to help but he was also cracked in the head and then taken. *Wequash* cried out "Father! Father! Please! No!" Her mother hugged her tight as the showering tears fell from her face and soaked the top of her daughter's head. Then *Mattawamp's* father *Anoosu* yelled out and walked forward. He was pushed back by the Mohegan who tells him, "Don't do it, it's hopeless, I know you are *PauWas*, but you must obey the English fathers or meet a painful death." *Anoosu* tried to push his way past *Sequnu* and said, "Then kill me now! Kill me now!" As some of Dandy's men head towards *Anoosu, Sequnu* moves his head side to side, silently telling them not to take this one. *Mattawamp* clinched his fist and teeth as his eyes watered over. *Kous* and his father stepped back and out of the way as the warriors were dragged away.

The Minister John Elliot ran over along with Nathaniel Curtis and other ministers. Minster Elliot said, "What in god's name is going on! This was not the accord! We are to baptize these poor creatures and save their souls lest they perish in hell for sorting with Satan. Why are they being taken away? I protest, stop this at once!"

Mr. Dandy walked to him and said with an unholy smile, "Why Minister Elliot, we are merely trying to detour and cleanse this dusky lot from any form of treachery or sinister revolt therein." The Minster shook his head at him and said, "And I'm sure you will yield a hefty profit for such 'cleansing' with your human cargo!" Dandy smirked and said, "Now, now minister, let's not be hasty. You worry about their souls and we shall protect his majesty's kingdom from the skulking devils so that our blessed land could be prosperous with god-fearing Christians." The Mohegan *Sequnu* took a brief interlude behind an oak tree nearby. He took a deep breath, sadly looked down, then pulled out a bottle of rum and took a vigorous swig. Just as he took his second guzzle, he was called out by the land speculator, Fredrick Whitmore. "*Sequnu! Sequnu!* Now where is that bloody Indian?" *Sequnu* tucked the bottle under his shirt and ran to Whitmore. "I am here, sir" They walked to the other side of the meeting house away from all the *Nipmuc* captives except for *Kous* and his father. They are sitting at a table outside with soldiers and colonist from Ipswich.

Fredrick Whitmore shook hands with the Ipswich colonists and said, "Good morrow my good ladies and gentlemen, everything is in place and *Sequnu* will help with the words." On the table was a deed for all the land at the beautiful village of *Wekabaug*. Whitmore said, "Now *Sequnu* explain to these two, if they sign this paper with some sort of mark they will be well taken care of here at the Praying Town." After *Sequnu* interpreted; *Kous*'s father spoke. *Sequnu* then said, "Sir, he asks what is the paper for and how does this seal a promise better than words?"

Whitmore looked at the colonist with an uneasy smile and said, "Tell them as chief we must obey their signature and protect them and their lands as we do our own king." *Kous's* father began to put a mark on the paper but he then slammed down the pen and shouted back at *Sequnu*. *Sequnu* looked tensely at Whitmore and said, "The *Nipmuc* told me he's not the chief and can't sign such a paper or make a promise for what he does not own." The colonist became restless and one of them said, "What's the problem Whitmore? We paid you a handsome sum for those lands, what is the issue here?" Whitmore squeezed his mouth together and put on a false smile and leaned in to talk with the man from Ipswich. "Like you sir, I am extremely vexed by these trivial procedures with these untamed brutes but ..."

Sequnu interrupts with news that *Kous* says he will sign the paper whether his father does or not. Whitmore grins and said, "Right there, boy; put your mark." *Kous* put his mark under the words *Chief of Wekabaug* and granted away all the land of *Wekabaug* to the people of Ipswich. Whitmore said, "Splendid-splendid, well done, boy! You'll be a trusty in no time ...chief!" He laughed and pats Kous on the head. Then he turned to the English guards and said, "All right then, take these two *Nipmuc* back to processing."

One of the Ipswich town leaders named Isaiah brought his wife along to the meeting. She gave her husband a modest hug and said, "This is marvelous me-lord! My heart hastens to be at our new settlement! They say it's well timbered with divers animals for hunting and sits by a handsome river!" Isaiah says. "Yes, love. And would you know, the savages would frolic about in the waters daily with scant fear of illness! What lunacy or primeval blood courses through them to permit such frequent wetting of the body?"

Back at the holding area, between the cries and confusion, the *Nipmucs* were processed and forced to their new quarters. They were handed a set of dingy English clothes and were forced to pile all their buckskin, feathers, medicine pouches and other sacred items into a fire pit. Nathaniel Curtis looked on with disgust when a tattered militiaman with rotten teeth named Jack walked up behind him. With an abrupt pat on the back he said, "Ha, ha, looks like the heathen attire is cooked to turn, aye. Ha ha!" Nathaniel hurled an angry look, then grabbed Jack tightly by the shirt and lifted him slightly from his feet. The Lieftenant witnessed the act and yelled to Nathaniel. "Release that man, Curtis!" Nathaniel lets loose Jack and stormed away. Jack showed his brown and chipped teeth while sporting a morbid chuckle and straightening his dirty shirt.

Meanwhile *Mattawamp* and his family were led to their new housing. *Mattawamp* strolled sadly as the outward part of them smolders away in the fire, their inner sprits left bereft and cold as the winter moon. They walked past the biggest structure at the fort and *Mattawamp* got a cold chill. He saw the crossed rods of his dream at the top of the structure his father and the other *PauWas* were holding. He stared so hard that he bumped into the front door of his new habitat.

The homes were flimsy, uncomfortable, and lined up like stables. *Wequash* and her mother went to their lonely hut as they wept wondering what happened to her father. One by one, the ministers and soldiers went to each dwelling to chop off all the hair of the boys and men. When they came to *Mattawamp's* house he watched as the men hacked off his father's hair and could feel the pain in his eyes. Then when he saw his own braids drop to the cracked and moldy floor, he felt his dreams and thoughts evaporate like dew before the morning sun. His mother had the same look on her face when her sister died three winters before.

A mile outside the prison sat a trading post and tavern where all the soldiers and militiamen socialized, traded and gathered. Wolf, bear, catamount and beaver skins were piled eight feet high before they were taken away and replaced with fresh ones. There were five soldiers standing outside by a tree stump practicing their musket fire. Their target was a nest of eagles in a tall pine tree. A wounded eagle attempted to escape while the soldier reloaded the musket. He yelled into the tree. "Keep still there you vermin and I shall ease your passing!" He took a big gulp of rum and finished off the bird. As the eagle tumbled to the earth the soldiers let out a big "Huzza! Huzza!" Inside the tavern, Jack with the rotten teeth was getting drunk with his friends. He said to one of his partners. "The nerve of that Curtis, he's more in league with the bloody savage than with the crown! How dare he! I'm not some upstart you know!" His older friend, who is also a raggedy and hairy looking soul, replied, "Don't mind him lad. You serve well, what you say we go get a taste of the local meat tonight, ha ha!" They smile with sinister grins to one another as they raised their mugs.

As the night wore on, the two men become extremely drunk and then they crept back to the "Praying Town." The men were lurking around the quarters of *Wequash* and her mother. The girl and her mother were huddled together on a frayed and worn bed. The two men crashed in and grabbed the mother. They both held her down and the older man covered her mouth to mute the screams. *Wequash* jumped in to try and help her mom and Jack punched her in the side of the head knocking her to the floor. Seeing her daughter on the floor in a daze; *Wequash's* mother struggled to get the hairy and dirty 200 pound man off her. The man struck her in the face and ribs several times as he tore off her clothes. He raped her and hit her repeatedly as Jack eyed *Wequash*.

Jack picked up the thirteen year-old injured girl and began removing her clothes. The older man yelled over to Jack and said, "Hey there lad, that one's a little young, let her bloom a bit more and have this one, ha, ha!" Jack yelled back as he continued undressing her. "Young says you! Ripe says I! I like my flowers fresh!" While Jack was talking, he didn't realize the older man had run out because Nathanial Curtis was charging in. Just before he could rape the girl, he felt a sword to his throat. Nathaniel shouted, "Release the girl or I shall run you through!" Just then other soldiers, a minister, and Captain Pierce hurried in. Jack was grabbed and apprehended and the other man was held outside. The soldiers were holding back Nathaniel from striking Jack. *Wequash's* mother was on the floor, eyes rolling back in her head and gurgling up blood from her internal injuries. Jack was dragged outside with the older man and the Minster stays in to tend to *Wequash* and her mother.

While both men were being detained, Captain Pierce castigated them. After ten minutes, the minister came out with information on *Wequash* and her mother. "The young girl is in a state of lassitude but should recover. However, the mother is dead, there's nothing we can do." Captain Pierce said to the two men, "It would appear, you two dregs have lost all manner of civility, that you would so much lust after these forest creatures and defile all sensibility as it were. Do not make yourself familiar with the heathen again. Perhaps two days in the stockade will afford you a more abstemious appetite for such imprudent deeds! Take them away and dispose of the body!" Nathaniel was fuming and said, "This is an outrage! These men should be hanged!" Captain Pierce said, "This is my ruling. Do not forget your place before such claims are hurled!" Nathaniel slammed his sword in the ground and said, "Blast your ruling man! What are we to do for these poor Indians that we have rained down our cursed presence and caused havoc and ruin upon every turn! Were we not charged with the duty to spread the gospel and justice? It is clear there is scant evidence of that, and these people should be returned to their villages lest our corruption of integrity damn us all! And your ruling sir; is not so grand that I'm certain, the good Lord did not bequeath you to be such a foul master!"

Captain Pierce was extremely upset at these words and shouted back, "How dare you, man, speak to me in such blasphemes tone; you are hereby extricated from this fort; no such insubordination shall linger on my watch!" Muskets were turned to Nathaniel as he was forced to leave. As he walked past the older rapist and murderer, he said, "You filthy ingrate! You despicable monster! That was the chief's wife you killed and raped. You are the devil here! You!" The murdering rapist conjured a depraved grin and said, "Aaah-Hail to the Queen. Ha, ha!" Nathanial punched the man in the face before he was expelled from the fort. The minister was told to put *Wequash* in another shack. She was put in with *Mattawamp* and his family.

She was wrapped in an old blanket when she was brought into the dwelling. *Mattawamp* and his parents ask what happened but the girl did not respond. She limped to a corner and curled into the fetal position and didn't utter a word.

The morning came and there was little time for *Mattawamp* or his family to ask *Wequash* where her mother was. Life at the Praying Town prison was agony heaped on misery. At first light the prisoners were brought to pray, then all the boys and men were put to work. The *Nipmuc* boys and girls that were too small to do heavy labor were sold off as house servants at new English settlements. The men, starting from age eleven, were taken off the Praying Town to cut timber to be shipped to England. It was dangerous work and loss of life and limb was common among the *Nipmuc* labor camp. Next, they were forced to toil for other town folk and help build their new settlements and plow new fields. All the women and young girls were separated to do their chores. They cooked, cleaned, sewed, washed clothes and harvested crops for the English. They were taught to work with pigs, cattle and take care of the Englishmen's horses. The *Nipmucs* were familiar with hard work except this time it didn't benefit any of them. To make matters worse, the Indians would attempt to sing *Nipmuc* chants while working to ease the toil but would be lashed with a horse whip or thrown in the stockade for doing so. They were forced to work in silence until they learned hymns from the gospel.

The Praying Town prison was built on the worst possible site for farming. The ground was rocky, dry and unfertile. Since the *Nipmucs* were not allowed to hunt, they had to survive on meager rations from the English. The cattle and pigs they tended to were for whites only. Amid all the work was the daily inculcation of the gospel. All the Nipmucs would gather on the ground under a tree as Minster Elliot shared his words. "Good morrow my children, I shall now conduct our daily blessing. O Lord of Grace, be thou guiding Spirit that I may be a beacon of light to a wicked and murky place; and unfetter these poor deceived souls who have conjured a dark reckoning all their days. Liberate their hearts, dear lord that they may discard their careless and lustful nature and reject the yoke of Satan. I trust in thee oh lord, that all your creatures are precious and even these piteous folk can be forgiven for their reckless and unchaste manner. Please, my lord, I ask you to exonerate these souls, for I believe despite their past there is hope to save them and bring them into a life of worship and civility."

As the words were being translated, *Mattawamp* was confused by what is said and his father *Anoosu* feels the need to say some words himself. *"Sequnu"* *Anoosu* calls out. "Tell this PauWas I would speak, please translate my words" *Anoosu* stands up and addresses Elliot. "You force us here under musket point, imprison us, then you speak of god? You say many words that speak to troubles which in all my years I have not witnessed. This *'Satan'* you speak of does not dwell here unless he came with you upon your giant ships. I am *Anoosu, PauWas* of the *Nipmuc,* Crow clan from the village of *Wekabaug* and the rivers and forest do not know you. I see the animals being cut down and slaughtered like the trees that are sent far away. I see other Indians foolish and empty from the strong drink you provide. Then I see the foul treatment, slavery, and abuse by your people and you speak of civility? I don't have the words to describe such greed and disregard for life; I reject your words and your god! You can imprison my body but my heart is free. It would do you good to learn our ways before your destructive habits end all life!"

Elliot took on an upset tone as the *Nipmucs* mumbled in concern to one another. Elliot said, "Dear child, once you have been baptized and quickened with the lord savoir … coupled with vigorous lessons, your bewitched mind will be cleansed from all your malignant thoughts!" Suddenly *Kous* stood up and said, "Dear Minister, we respect and honor our English fathers, don't listen to him; I am *Kous* the new chief." *Anoosu* and the other *Nipmucs* balk at his words. *Mattawamp* shouted to *Kous* and said, "What are you talking about? You're a traitor to your people, and no chief! You are no more than a crumb let alone chief!" *Kous* looked at *Mattawamp* and yelled back "I am Chief, I signed the English paper that says so!" *Kous's* mother and father sit sadly and appear very ill; there are small red bumps beginning to appear on them. Soldiers came and calmed the disruption as John Elliot continues his sermon.

Each day flowed the same; like tainted salt into a dark pit that dries hearts and preserves bitterness. *Mattawamp* ached for his home as the winter months set in. *Wequash* revealed what happened to her mother and this added to their sorrow. *Nipmucs* were beaten and hanged from time to time for singing or dancing. John Elliot was working on a dictionary and bible in the *Nipmuc* language even as he worked to eradicate this native language. By the early spring, *Kous's* parents have both died of small pox along with 132 others. *Kous*, on the other hand, has become a trusty and is even allowed to carry a sword. *Kous* is more brutal on his people than the English and many times he was the one to report "heathen activity." And just as the flowers were blooming, *Mattawamp's* mother collapsed from fever as she worked the fields. She was carried back to her hut and put to bed. When *Mattawamp* and *Anoosu* returned from labor camp, they see her sweating profusely as *Wequash* tries to keep her cool. But her skin is showing signs of the red lesions and death is upon her.

Two days later, she was still in bed and was much worse. *Mattawamp* and his father refused to leave her side and had to be forced by musket point to do the morning work and prayers. Upon their return they could see her life fading fast. *Anoosu* kneels beside her with tears in his eyes. He reached under his shirt and pulled out an eagle feather he picked up from the labor site. He started to cry as he waved the feather over his wife and began a *Nipmuc* chant. *Mattawamp* and *Wequash* soon join in and the song gets louder. Shortly after, *Kous* barges in to interrupt the song and yelled at them using the few English phrases he learned. *Mattawamp* gave him a sharp look and spoke back in *Nipmuc*, saying, "Don't use those words with us! You sound like a choking duck – now, get out, you traitor!" *Kous* sighed and returned to speak *Nipmuc* and says, "Stop this stupid singing at once – you know it's forbidden, we are to be as our English fathers; besides... she will die soon ... like the rest of them ... like my parents." *Mattawamp* said, "We will not stop, this is who we are, and we have not forgotten! But I can see from your fine English clothes and English words you have!" *Kous* pulled out his sword and held it up. *Mattawamp* started to rise but his father held him back. *Anoosu* looked sadly at *Kous* and said, "Have you no shame? Have you no shame at all?"

Kous slowly looked down at the floor and then put the sword away. Before *Kous* walks out he said, "Remember, I warned you to stop!" *Anoosu* resumed the song and *Wequash* and *Mattawamp* tried to comfort the woman in her final moments. About an hour later, the door was smashed open. Two soldiers came crashing in, one with a musket and the other with a sword. It was Jack and the older man – the same two who raped and killed *Wequash's* mother and almost raped her. When *Wequash* saw the men, she went into a state of panic and wet her dress. Jack smashed the musket in *Anoosu's* face, breaking his teeth. As the blood spattered around, the older man put a rope around his neck and begins to drag him out. *Mattawamp* was held back by sword point. Jack said to *Mattawamp*, "Make one move, savage, and I'll skewer you like a swine!" As *Anoosu* squirmed and fought for air, he said to *Mattawamp* "Don't worry, son! Just stay with your mother. I love you!" The two men took off with *Anoosu* as *Mattawamp* cried besides his mother. He was stricken with anxiety, worrying about where they were taking his father but also being with his dying mother. She died two hours later. *Mattawamp* wiped the tears from his face, took a deep breath, and snuck out to search for his father. He quietly searched the Praying Town, careful not to be seen. When he got in front of the church, he saw a grizzly sight! It was his father's head stuck on a pole in front of the church. As he watched the blood that still ran down the pole, he felt as if he jumped in an icy lake. Then fire gripped his heart like thunder shaking the sky. Nearby he saw the two men who killed his father. They were sitting by a small fire drinking rum and laughing. Jack said to the older man, "I'd say he officially failed bible study – ha, ha!" Mattawamp started shaking and went into a fit of rage. He saw a large rock on the ground, picked it up, and walked toward the men from the rear. With the same arms that have been chopping timber, hauling lumber, and working the fields for the past eight months, he slammed the big rock on Jack's head. Jack's skull is shattered and before his body crumbles to the ground, he was dead.

The older man pulled out his sword and attacked *Mattawamp.* The old man swings and misses, for the agile teen was too swift for the drunken soldier. *Mattawamp* dodged and swayed as the man chased him around the fire. Then the old man rapidly thrust his sword at *Mattawamp* but trips and eats his own blade through the neck. *Mattawamp's* eyes open wide at the sight of the impaled man and bloody mess of the other soldier. For a moment, he felt frozen in time. With his mother and father dead and the fact two Englishmen were dead, he knew he had to get out of the Praying Town. The only thing he had to do before he escaped was to take *Wequash* with him! He ran back to his quarters and told *Wequash* as he was breathing heavy. "Hurry – no time for questions! We have to leave now!" As they were preparing to leave, *Kous* ran in with his sword drawn. *Kous* said, "Stop right there!" As he pointed the sword at *Wequash*. *Kous* then said, "Both of you follow me and don't make a sudden move or sound!" *Mattawamp* didn't want to try anything out of fear *Kous* would kill *Wequash* so he did as he was told. In the dark of night, *Kous* led them up past the church, then by the meeting house. He then took them to the edge of the far side of the fort. There was a small gate there that was used by soldiers to come in and out in case of an attack. *Kous* unlocked the gate and said, "Go!" *Mattawamp* had a look of surprise and said, "But..." Kous cuts back in and said, "Hey-no time for kisses it will be dawn soon, now go!" *Mattawamp* said to Kous, "Come with us!" *Kous* slowly replies with a hollow look on his face. "No...this is my life now." *Kous* and *Mattawamp* don't shake hands but they do exchange a nod. *Mattawamp* and *Wequash* then take off in the night. They move like the wind as they cross hills, thickets, and swamps. Running, running, running. Abruptly, *Mattawamp* falls to his knees, not from exhaustion but in tears. He was thinking about the image of his father, and losing his mother, but what really bothered him is that he killed someone. *Mattawamp* started to vomit and wail. *Wequash* cradled him in her arms like a new born baby as the tears flowed from his eyes. Fearing soldiers may be coming; *Mattawamp* pulled himself together and said, "We have to keep moving!"

They ran until the sun rose and moved cautiously by day. They were finally at the shores of the Great Winding River.

It was spring and the water is rougher than before. But *Mattawamp* is stronger and has the will of the eagle, bear, and crow combined. *Wequash* looked at the heavy rapids nervously and *Mattawamp* said, "Don't worry, I will carry you!" She held on tight as *Mattawamp* paddled the rapids with his strong arms. There was no fear of sturgeon grabbing his hair because there was only stubble left on his head. With all his power he fought the water and won, but by the time they made it to shore he is exhausted. As he caught his breath he looked around. He jumped up and ran toward something. *Wequash* asked, "What's wrong?" As she chased after him. It was the Pocumtuc village, a place that had sat alongside the long river for ten thousand years. The village was now completely abandoned. Those who survived moved on to seek out other clans up north. *Mattawamp* shook his head in grief and they moved on. By dusk, they reached the spot *Mattawamp* was searching for. It was the place he had his vision journey. *Mattawamp* and *Wequash* looked at each other with sad eyes. Then out of the woods came the Mohawk *Tso Ka'We* he met long ago. He was very thin, alone, and had a somber look about him. He walked over to *Mattawamp* and handed him back the moose carved knife.

⌘　⌘　⌘

Deadly Deeds

❦

They're coming for me!

I hope this letter is found in time so this doesn't happen again to someone else. When you do find this, my body will be long gone, like a crumpled leaf after the fall, but I bestow you with this urgent warning I am leaving behind. I don't have much time but I'll try to explain how it all started. Please be cautious as you read my words! Take a moment to look around lest you make the same mistake I did.

It all began a year ago when I leased a small cottage in the western part of the state. It was a quaint and sturdy home with a beautiful throw rug, fine leather couch, fireplace, and charming country kitchen. The cottage sat behind a large mountain and just off the main road that led to town. In the front of the house, left of the cobble stone walkway, was a nice little wicker table and chair. Behind it was a beautiful hiking trail and bike path that crisscrossed a little brook. Also, from the back window you could see the small swampy pond full of tall grass, frogs and an occasional heron stopping in to wet its beak.

Each morning I would start off the day with a good stretch and brisk run and then come indoors for a glass of juice, eggs and toast with pepper on the eggs – no salt, thanks. Then in the afternoon, I would drive into town to pick up the paper and get a coffee. The strange looks didn't start right away. Well, maybe they did because I noticed them twisting their heads away from my eyes from day one.

But it wasn't until four weeks had passed that I really got the creeps from the town folk. Instead of rotating their faces away they openly gawked at me. I did my best to walk away with my paper and coffee but their looks were on me like moss to a pond-side stone. That's when my troubles began. My tranquil nights in this country paradise turned into a horror of shrieking sounds. All night long they howled like angry jackals returning from the slaughter. Then this one night was the worst. I was trying to get through the evening by plugging my ears and taking my mind off it with a good book. I made a big cup of *Atepen* tea and tried to relax. I drifted to sleep while reading *Mann's Gourmet Fish Recipes* but then I was awakened by a loud bang on the back door. I took a look around carefully before I even moved. I tiptoed to the door but dared not open it, so instead I looked out the window.

I wiped the mist off the pane and looked out across the swampy pond. It was dark and foggy like gray milk poured into the air. Contemplating who or what could be outside gripped my soul like a hungry vice clutching a bone. Then suddenly a bang came from the front door! I pounced toward the front and nearly tripped running to see what it was. I didn't open the door for I could feel an intense presence coupled with heavy breathing on the other side. I reluctantly peeped through the peephole but there was something blocking my view. "I bet it's those bitches and bastards from town," I thought. The dirty glances were over, now they wanted action, I figured! So I ran down to the basement to get away. I made it just in time because they tore their way in just as I twisted the basement door locked! I could hear them walking around upstairs and talking to one another but it wasn't in my language.

They were knocking things over, trashing the place and stuffing their mouths with all my food! "They should be put back in chains and returned to their master!" I said to myself! Finally they left and I went stealthily up the stairs. As suspected, my place was a mess. My fine leather couch was torn to shreds. They stole my throw rug, pissed and shit all over the floor, and emptied my fridge.

Yes, I'm the fool because I should have left right then. But I'm very stubborn and I didn't want to break the one-year lease so I thought I could ride it out. This malice, threats on my life, and destruction of my place went on for months and months and only got worse. I went to the local police but they were one of them so it was no use. Last week they stole my car so now I'm on foot!

Now, here I am one year later and the lease ends today. I made it, or so I thought. I had not looked at the lease since I moved in and apparently hadn't read all the fine print. As I read the fine print, I freaked out so bad I coughed up hair! It states:

"We the citizens and the town of Dinac shall only lease and rent to our kind. All others may stay for a respite but must depart after four weeks. Those who choose to stay past that time period risk life and limb. All those who stay one year shall be eaten!"

So, do you see my dilemma? I'm not a *"Dinac,"* I'm a *"Namtac!"* Those *Dinac's* have been barking and chasing my kind for centuries! We scratch and fight but I'm stranded and outnumbered! I hear them coming! So, please, read your lease well lest you end up renting from a bunch of dogs!

⌘ ⌘ ⌘

The Basket

☯

Webster, Massachusetts 1910. Lester and Rainy Corn Leaf and their four children, Daisy, Little Rainy, William and Lester Jr. were one of the few remaining Nipmuc families living on a small hill above the lake in the tiny mill town. To get by, they farmed, raised livestock, and sold handmade brooms. But most importantly of all, they made precious, woven baskets.

Some baskets were made from split ash and porcupine quills. Other styles included birch bark interwoven with cedar. They also designed some from sweetgrass and deer hair. Meticulously hand woven; interspersed with natural dyes and earth tones of Nipmuc tribal symbols, they were a big hit with the white town folk. But what's more, these baskets carried a sacred significance to the Nipmuc that connected them to the spirit world and their ancestors.

The grandmother of the four children made a very distinctive basket for them just before she died. She wanted to leave a unique gift behind so she made them a basket like no other. She started with the finest split brown ash from the mixed hardwood forests surrounding their home that she could find. The 81 year-old Elder pounded out the ash until she was able to get the desired strips for her basket. She recited an old Nipmuc prayer and poured her love into each row as she laced the beautiful bowl-style basket with red-dyed porcupine quills. The resilient quills were fashioned into a thunderbird on the front of the basket. Then, she wove intricate spiraled patterns around the sides. Around the top she wrapped freshly twisted and braided sweetgrass to give the basket additional blessing and beauty.

On the bottom of the basket she did something extra special. The Elder braided a long piece of her own hair and then cut it off. She took the braid and appliqued it into the bottom of the basket in the shape of a heart. This would keep her thoughts connected to her grandchildren even from the spirit world. An equally fine cover with a braided sweet grass bow handle was made to cover the sacred items that would be put inside. Within, were four wampum carvings to make a necklace representing their personal totems. Salmon, Crow, Turtle, and Bear effigies were the fine and detailed work of their uncle Tall Moose who moved to a reservation near Val D'Or, Quebec.

Everyone in the family was amazed at Tall Moose's gorgeous work and how he made the wampum come to life. Even though he went blind at the age of thirty from a drinking accident, his craftsmanship just got better over the years. Also inside this sacred container was a twist of tobacco and a round, smooth black stone added by their father Lester. He had picked up the stone from the shores of Deer Island on Boston Harbor during a ceremony honoring the Nipmuc people who perished during their internment of 1675. Lester kept that stone as a reminder of the sacrifice and suffering of their people, but also so that his family never forgot where they came from. In addition, their mom added a red tailed hawk feather she was gifted as a young girl, and a pouch of cedar. The basket was so beautiful and had a blissful glow about it. It contained all the elements of the spirit and the physical world and the weaves and patterns tied this family together in love and tradition. The basket sat on the top shelf in the kitchen above the canning jars and baking tins. Every now and then when the kids would get into a scuffle, Lester and Rainy would point to the basket as a reminder. They would have them recall the love and unity they must have for one another. "Like the basket, you are tied together to make something stronger." They said to their kids.

After the prompt, the children would hug and reflect in appreciation for what their grandmother left them. They would also think about the special gifts inside. Once the children grew up, they would remove their sacred belongings to start their own families. But that day never came. One beautiful Sunday morning the kids were playing their favorite game at the lake to cool off from the summer heat. They would swing into the water from a high ridge off the big oak tree to see who could land the furthest. At that same moment back at their home, there was a soft knock at their door. It was government agents from Indian affairs and they came to extract the children and ship them off to Indian Boarding School.

Their father tried to plead and reason with the agents. He told them, "Children need to be with their own parents. We love our children, please! Please! Don't take them away." They wouldn't listen, so he grabbed one of the agents by the shirt and shouted, "Get the hell out of my home! This is my family! We haven't done anything wrong, how can you do this to people!" As the children headed up the hill they noticed a big commotion by their front door and saw their dad face down on the ground in handcuffs. They all began to run toward their home to the sound of their mother screaming like she was on fire! "Nooo! Let him go! Let him go!" She cried. As they arrived they all reached down to get their father off the ground but were pulled away by the agents. One agent said with a loud and derisive murmur as his teeth clinched his cigar. "He's fine, settle down! There! There! How you kids be? My name is Donald McGreevy from Injun Affairs, and ya now gonna get the proper schoolin' ya needs. Ya gonna get a ride in a Model T, see, bet ya never did that before!"

One by one the children were forced into the vehicle as their mother and father screamed for somebody in the world to help them. "Don't worry" said another agent, "they will now be properly schooled and raised as good Christian folk!" In the blink of an eye the Corn Leafs' life had become dismal and shattered.

During the first three years of the state abduction, the parents were not allowed any contact with the kids. Their mother could feel their pain which ate her up from the inside. She slipped into a deep depression and was taken by the state to a vile and brutal insane asylum. Although she was not physically at the boarding school her senses were correct. All four of her children were beaten and molested on a routine basis. The place was more comparable to an adolescent concentration camp than a "school". They were taught to hate their brown skin and anything to do with their culture or tradition. The children were at the mercy of these insensitive strangers whose goal was to evaporate their souls, then refill it with a morbid self contempt.

When their mom died in the asylum of "unknown causes" in November of 1913, the children weren't notified until March the following year. The father, now completely alone, began to bury himself in a whiskey bottle. He continued his battle with Indian Affairs to get his children back but to no avail. He sold off the livestock and the crops became fallow. The house became dilapidated and unkempt. Each day he would walk down the hill and sit under the big oak tree by the lake shore where his children would play and swim. He would cry for his wife and children. On one occasion a sailboat passed him on the lake and a person shouted "Hey Injun, get your drunken ass off our beach!" Then another person threw a bottle at him hitting him in the head. As the blood dripped down the side of his face he jumped up and yelled back at them. "Your lake!? Your Lake!? We have always been here, you son of a bitches, this is MY lake!!" Suddenly Lester began to pound on the side of a tree and sang a Nipmuc war song. He sang for an hour and then headed to the liquor store.

When he got to the store the clerk said, "Lester, we're not selling any booze to you! I told you not to come back here!" He replied in a loud voice "Don't come back!? Get off my Lake!? – You people forget everything!! Even this store is on my great uncle's burial ground! When will *YOU get* out, huh!?"

Lester pointed across the field and said, "You see that over there!? Our village stood there since the beginning of all things! Then you showed up! You showed up! Not me!! You hear me?! Not me!!" Lester knocked over a shelf and yelled "Give me a goddamn bottle!" The clerk yelled back, "Get the hell out of my store! Here! Take it! Take it! Here's you damn bottle! Have two! Don't come back or I'll call the cops, see!"

While walking home, Lester drank one of the 100 proof bottles. He got home and staggered through the door. He looked into the vacant bedrooms of his children and for a moment he could hear their voices as they laughed and played. A smile mixed with tears came over his heavy face. He walked into his bedroom and stared at the side of the bed where his wife slept. He squeezed his eyes tightly while taking a huge breath of air as if he was emerging from deep water. He then cracked open the second bottle of whisky, took a big swig, and headed back to the kitchen. He sat there and mournfully stared up at the basket, that special basket. Suddenly there came a second pain in his heart, and then everything went dark. The police didn't find his body until three days later.

Shortly afterwards, the state confiscated the land, the house and everything in it, including the basket. The Indian agent Donald McGreevy stole the basket for his personal collection and kept it locked in his basement. He was reluctant to show it around through the years even though he adored it like a hunting trophy. It was stored inside a wooden bottle crate under his work shelf. The basket sat smothered, isolated and dark with only the cob webs and shadow as witness to its pain. McGreevy died at the age of fifty-six of neurosyphilis. He spent the remaining decade of his life in a sanatorium. Most of the time, he was heavily tranquilized due to his violent fits and delusions. When that didn't work he was put in isolation and in a strait jacket.

Since none of McGreevy's family came to visit him, he spent his days drooling on himself and talking to the urine-stained concrete walls. Soon after he died his son took possession of the basket and eventually passed it down to his son Fred. Many decades passed and the basket still remained isolated and away from its people.

Springfield, Massachusetts, 1989. Fred has no idea where his grandfather got the basket, but he was aware it is valuable and was looking to sell it. He checked the yellow pages and asked around for local Indian artifact collectors. He finally came across one Jeff Tarver. Tarver is a shady and unethical Indian artifact dealer who drove a big fancy car. He had been fined several times and even served three months' probation for selling Native American skulls and for grave robbing. Now he ran a small, secretly held business out of his home. Fred got Tarver on the phone and said, "Hello, my name is Fred McGreevy and I have this Indian basket I inherited and I believe it to be very valuable." Tarver replied, "Well hello there! Thanks for your call! How old is the basket? Where is it from?" Fred said, "Well... it has all these red designs woven into it with some kind of odd material. The basket itself is made from strips of a tree weaved in and out very tight and strong. The front has a bird symbol but I have no idea where it's from. It's very old and has a lid that I tried to take off but seems to be bonded on over the years. The bottom of it has some kind of hair, probably from a horse, shaped in a heart. I tell you this, it's really pretty and I hate to part with it but I need to buy a new snow blower before the winter comes."

Tarver said, "Humm.... Well ok, sounds good! I'll come over and take a look at it!" He arrived a few hours later at Fred's home to view the basket. As soon as Tarver eyed the basket he immediately realized that it was one of a kind and extremely valuable but was not going to let Fred know. Tarver nonchalantly looked at the basket and said, "Well, I seen many like this before, they're not worth much, but I'd be willing to help you out. And you say this hasn't been opened?" Fred excitingly said, "No, but like I said, I tried and it was ..." Tarver abruptly cut him off because he got the information he wanted.

He knew there could be even greater treasure inside. "I just have to convince this sucker not to open it," he thought to himself. "Oh, good, Mr. McGreevy!" he said with a grin. "You don't want to open up such an old relic, you could ruin it. Then instead of being worth two hundred bucks it would be worth fifty." Fred scratched his head and said, "Two hundred? I thought it would be worth more, like four or five hundred." Tarver internalized his devilish glee because he knew the basket was easily worth eight to ten thousand dollars. Further, whatever was inside could double that. Jeff

Tarver was like a starving swine drooling over a trough. He had to have the basket. "Ok, Mr. McGreevy, I'm in a generous mood. I'll give you $350.00 right here and right now!" Fred only paused for a moment and then jumped at the cash. "Ok, sure I'll take it, thanks Mr. Tarver!" Seconds later they were pumping hands and Jeff Tarver was out the door. As he carefully secured the basket in the trunk of his fancy new Lincoln, he whispered to the basket, "You are gonna make me a ton of cash. Yea, baby, yea!"

While heading back to his nice suburban town on the other side of the state he got lost in Springfield. Tarver ended up in the most drug infested, crime-ridden ghettos of the city. He noticed the air was suddenly filled with loud rap music coupled with the faint and repetitive cry of police sirens off in the distance. The thumping and rough cadence serenaded the rows of vacant buildings, pushers and users probing the streets. Tarver looked around nervously as the hard stares of the youths were directed at his fancy new car. He would have blown through the red light ahead but there was a car already stopped. It was a gold Trans Am with primer on the front quarter panel. The rear window vibrated from the music inside.

Outside of the car three men were chatting to the driver. Tarver looked cautiously but turned away in order not to make eye contact with the guys. He slipped up for a second and locked eyes with one of the men. The man yelled to Tarver and said, "What, motha fucka? What? You wanna go? You wait till 'um done talkin', bitch!" Tarver quickly looked at the floor of his car. The man then laughed loudly with his friends and went back to his conversation. They talked for another ten minutes before the Trans Am drove off. As one of the men walked away, he grabbed his crotch and gestured to Tarver while giving him the middle finger with the other hand. Then the man yelled out, "Get yo peckerwood ass up out of here before you gets done!" Tarver pulled into the nearest gas station seeking refuge and directions to the highway. The moment he was inside, two young men stole his car. He ran out and yelled to the thieves, "Hey! Hey! That's my car!" The driver yelled back, "It's mine now, Cracka! Nice car, mother fucka! Ha, ha, ha!" Tarver chased after the car while screaming, "Come back- come back! The driver replied, "Yea bitch! Catch me! Ha ha!" The driver slowed down then sped up, taunting him as he hopelessly tried to catch the car. Tarver only made it two blocks before he became exhausted. Then the driver says to his partner, "See, nigga! I told you we could do it," as they peel off, leaving Tarver in the middle of the ghetto. Shortly afterward, Tarver was beaten up and stripped of his clothes by two crack heads. The police discovered him an hour later all black and blue and wearing only his boxers. By this time, his nice fancy car was at a secret garage getting chopped up.

The young man driving the stolen car was 17 year-old Eric Vaughn and was known on the street as E. On the passenger side is 17 year-old Todd Conlee, known as TC. They were good friends and both came from impoverished homes. E had a large family and dreamed of being a basketball star. TC had no siblings and lived alone with his mother. He has no idea or direction of what he wants to do with his life. He focused mostly on supplying himself with weed and helping his mom pay bills. As they both surveyed the contents of the car and took what they wanted, E opened the trunk.

He saw the basket and said, "Yo, my nigga, TC! Check this shit out! Wow! This shit is phat! This is like one of them Indian baskets I seen on TV and shit! Hey, TC, ain't you Indian?" TC gave him a half smile and looked away and said, "Uh ... yea, my mom's Indian."

E gave his buddy a sarcastic look and said, "Well, you is too, fool! What kind of basket is this ?" TC looked at the basket and then looked away as if in pain and said, "Yo, dog! I don't know nothing about that stuff!"

E replied and said, "You should take this shit home!" TC looked away and said, "Nah- nigga, you keep it." E said, "Hey, now! What I tell ya about dat? You too high-yellow to be callin' me nigga," he said with a laugh. TC replied, "Ah- Fuck you!" Both of them broke out laughing. As the teens each received $350.00 for the car, E picked up the basket and said with a more serious tone, "Yo my nigga, really, you should take it." TC looked at his friend and then stared at the basket for a moment and said, "Sure, whatever man, I'll take it. I can use it to hold my weed and cash." After a quick stop at the reefer house, TC made it back to his housing complex.

When he got home, his mom was sitting on a plastic-covered couch smoking a cigarette watching the news. She got off work a few hours before but still has on her super-market uniform. Her long black hair was pinned up in a bun with loose hair strands waving over her brown eyes. Margret Conlee bore TC at a young age and was herself raised in foster homes. TC's father walked out on him before he was born and Margret has been struggling alone ever since. TC tossed $160.00 in her lap and said with a smile, "Hey, ma! Now we can get the phones on!" She picked up the money gratefully but then made a stern face and said, "I swear to god, Todd – if you did anything stupid ..."

She stopped in mid-sentence when she noticed him holding the basket under his arm. Her eyes flickered and she was enthralled at the sight but then appeared angry. She pushed her hair strands away from her face and took a hard drag on her cigarette and said, "Where did you get that?" TC quickly and nervously replied, "Uh... It's nothing. Eric found this and thought I would like it. He begged me to take it so I said what the hell."

"Watch your language, young man!" She said abruptly. TC put his head down with a soft smile and said, "Sorry, ma, but it is pretty cool, you wanna hold it? She quickly said, "No!" Margret's eyes began to water as she stared at the basket. "Ma, what is it? What's wrong?" She wiped her tears and got up and hugged her son and said, "I don't know, I'm okay. Why don't you go eat, I made rice and chicken." After TC ate, he went to his room and put the basket on top of his dresser across from his bed. He got in his bed and put on his headphones. As the rap music blared in his ears, his eyes were fixed on the basket.

He reached into his pockets and pulled out $72.00 and a small bag of marijuana. TC looked at the cash and pot, and then looked at the basket. He walked over to the basket and picked it up. He examined it up and down, then stared at the bottom. Gently, he traced his fingers along the heart shape of hair. After setting it back down, TC tried to open it. At first it was difficult but then it released itself to him. When he removed the cover, a hollow breeze shot through his room. The hair on the back of his neck stood up as he was overtaken by a weird feeling. He felt a little dizzy and sat on the edge of his bed. After a few moments, he got back up and walked toward the basket. With the cover off, he slowly put his hand inside. The hawk feather, tobacco and cedar had disintegrated; only the wampum and black stone remained. TC slowly took out each piece of wampum and the black stone. He studied the pieces as if he were a jeweler. The Basket began to have a misty glow coming from the inside. TC felt drawn to the Basket and slowly put his face near for a better view.

Tensely, he moved closer and closer till his face disappeared inside. Suddenly, Todd Conlee began to hear the sound of drums. His heart started to beat faster and the light from the Basket ignited a fire in his spirit ... Todd is flying and tasting the stars. He sees a cornfield and it is bright as citrus sunshine. Todd is surrounded by flashes and blurs, like a majestic firework display of places he's never been. He's mesmerized by an exalted peace. Then he's by a shimmering lake and notices a dugout canoe traversing by. There are people inside who know him. A red tailed hawk is circling overhead. Her wings are illuminated like neon fire. There's a hazy image of an elderly woman standing beside him. To the right there's children laughing and swinging off a tree into the water. One of the kids notices Todd and smiles softly at him. Then the child beckons him to join in on the fun. Todd joyfully walks toward the swing.

Abruptly, though, an ambulance screaming up Main St. pulled him back to his room. Todd fell to the floor in complete exhaustion. For a moment he was totally confused and looked around as if lost; six hours had passed and the sun was rising. Todd looked at the bag of marijuana with his eyes wide open. Even though he hadn't smoked any, he threw the bag in the trash. He again focused on the Basket. He observed it as if it was an animal freed from a cage, expecting it to jump at him. The cacophony of the city streets diverted his attention once again. He headed off to school, walking backwards out of his room, never taking his vision off the Basket.

After school TC found himself in a place he's never been, the city library. After getting lost amongst the valley of books, he finally found the tiny Native American section in the back by the old radiator with the paint peeled off. Following his search through four books, he finds a Basket similar to his. Not only does he find that the Basket is made by the Nipmuc people, he read of the travesty and abuses Native Americans have suffered. He read how in 1675 thousands of Christianized Indians, actual allies of the settlers, were taken from their homes and left to die in a place called Deer Island in

Boston Harbor. Tribe after Tribe, Massacre after massacre; he learned of the abominable horrors people like him had gone through. Todd was captivated by the new information but was filled with an anger and sadness like never before. He picked up another book entitled *"Pow Wows across Turtle Island."* The magnificent outfits of the regalia the people wore seem to leap off the pages and into Grand Entry. The photographs abound with beautiful Eagle Bustles, Jingle Dresses and Fancy Shawl outfits. On the next page he finds that he likes the Porcupine Roach headdress with the hawk feather coming out the side.

He smiled and a sense of familiar nostalgia overtook him as he turned each page. When he came to the Eastern Woodland section, he noticed a handsome buckskin outfit with symbols on it matching his Basket. He got excited with a visceral connection to what he had felt and witnessed. He wanted to feel more.

With several books in hand, he zipped home through his coarse neighborhood. When he got home, his mom was sitting on the plastic covered couch smoking a cigarette watching the news. She got off work a few hours before but still is wearing her supermarket uniform. Her long black hair is again pinned up. He set the books down on the table next to the ashtray and said, "Hey, Mom, can we talk?" She swiftly replies "Look honey, I couldn't turn the phones on yet. The rent was three weeks late and...." He cut her off and said, "No-no, it's not that! Something happened to me last night, and shit... Sorry, I mean. I can't explain it in words but...can you take me to a pow wow? I want to see if I can find someone to tell me more about the Basket. I can't explain why, but I need to know." She pushed her hair strands away from her face and took another hard drag on her cigarette and looked deeply at her son. Instead of saying a word she got up, fighting off her tears until she made it to the bathroom.

Todd stood there with a look of concern. Five minutes later she returned still wiping her eyes dry. She softly said to her son, "All my life I wanted to know who I was. I lived with so many white people I thought I was white. But there would always be someone there to remind me that I'm not one of them, or I don't fit in. I wanted to be part of the Indian ways so bad, but I didn't know the first thing about it. After a while I just became afraid because I didn't think they would accept me anyways. Then you came home with that Basket. I felt something, too, that I can't explain. It's like that Basket is calling me home." She gave her son a big hug. Todd said, "Does this mean we're going?"

She wiped her tears and said, "Yes! We're going to do this together!" The following week they went off to a pow wow for the first time. They went to the Nipmuc Grand Pow wow in Central Massachusetts. As they got out of the car they were greeted by the sounds of the drums and the MC of the Pow Wow saying over the microphone "OK! All Smoke Dancers, you're up next!"

The gentle smell of sweet grass and cedar filled the air. Men, women and children were passing by in stunning regalia, throwing smiles and nods their way. Some were running as they tightened their headdresses and feathers to make it to the circle on time. Todd was proudly holding the Basket as his mom walked closely beside him. Once they arrived at the entrance, they saw a big Indian man with shades on named High Crow. What stands out about him to Todd is the man's blue bandana, two long braids and denim jacket. He smiled at Todd and his mom and said, "Welcome!"

A sense of ease comes over Margret and Todd but they stand there not knowing what to do next. High Crow said, "Well come on in! We are all family here! Holy ... son! Where did you get that there Basket?" Todd said, "Well, we came to find out more about it. Could you tell me anything at all?"

High Crow took off his shades, rubbed his chin, and said, "That's one of the old ones. Real special. It's Nipmuc. For something like that you should go show that to the Nipmuc Elders at the Elders' tent." He led the way past the fry bread hut and the wampum makers' table. As Todd walked through the grounds, he noticed guys his age wearing their hair very long and singing around a big drum. They look so happy and so proud, he thought to himself.

When they entered the Elders' tent, High Crow pointed out a very old man in the back smoking a pipe and wearing a faded and worn-down Stetson hat. He said, "Right over there! That is Lester Corn Leaf Jr., one of the oldest around; I think he's about 92 or 93, I'm not sure really. Let me take ya to him!" Lester was facing the other direction when they approached him. Margret and Todd looked at his long, gray braided hair going down the back of his red flannel shirt. He appeared preoccupied and distant within his own thoughts. High Crow said to Lester, "Excuse me, Les, these folks got something you ought to look at." Lester puffed on his pipe and then slowly turned around. His eyes went straight to the Basket. Margret began the conversation telling him about her son and the Basket. Lester is not hearing what she is saying. Her words are like a soft hymn being overtaken by the thundering drums of recollection. He can see his father waving to him from the cornfield. His big sister Daisy is running up the hill with blueberries. His mind flashes to his brother William and sister Little Rainy. They are sitting on the porch watching uncle Tall Moose carve wampum while grandma is making Baskets. His mother is calling him in to eat. "Lester. Lester? "Excuse me, Mr. Corn Leaf? So, can you tell me anything about this Basket?" said Margaret with anticipation.

Lester Jr. closed his eyes for a moment, and then he reached for his walking stick. It had a turtle carved on top.

The frail old man pulled himself up and walked toward the Basket. He held it in his hands and a smile of relief took over his face. Soon the smile turned into a fragile laugh. Lester Jr. then began to weep and fell to his knees. High Crow and Todd helped him back to his chair. Lester Jr. makes eye contact with Todd and Margret. He stares at them both intensely. He looks up at the Sky and lets out a loud "Thank you Creator!" coupled with tears. Lester Jr. finally speaks to Todd and Margret.

He spoke slowly and his voice was soft and gravelly so they have to move in close to hear his words. "I was just.... 11 years old when they came and took me to that there boarding school. We sure had a hard time of it. My sister Little Rainy and brother William never made it out of there, nope. Me and Daisy ... well, we made it out....... what was left of us anyways. After that I went and fought for this country. I joined the United States Army. I wanted to get as far away as possible. But this Nipmuc land called me back. I came home and got married, we had a daughter. When my wife died of cancer I had to raise my daughter alone. She was a strong and beautiful girl. She tried to help me but I was just drinking too much so she kept running away, till one day she never came home. When I got sober I tried to find her and never stopped looking for her. Later on I found out she died giving birth to a little girl and the baby was taken by the state. I prayed and prayed to find that little girl. I've been searching all my days and I asked Creator before you take me, please let me find my granddaughter. And today.... the Basket comes back to me. That Basket my grandma made for us so long ago. She told us it was special."

Two weeks later, uncovered records confirmed that Lester Corn Leaf Jr. is indeed the grandfather of Margret Conlee. When she was born the state decided to change her last name to Conlee and concealed her true identity. Soon afterward they were reunited with all their family. They meet all 27 descendants of Daisy Corn Leaf along with hundreds of other Nipmuc people. Todd and his mom's hearts soared with joy. They moved out of the city and started a new life among their Tribe and changed their name back to Corn Leaf. Lester Corn Leaf Jr. lived another two years. Todd and Margret spent every moment they could loving, sharing and learning from their Elder.

Today, Margaret Corn Leaf is the director of the Nipmuc tribal daycare center and is running for tribal council. Todd Corn Leaf never stole again and put all his focus on school and his tribe. Presently he has a Master's degree in Native American history and Anthropology. He gives lectures and workshops on Native history throughout the United States and Canada and works with other tribes. Most of his work has to do with the protection of Native graves, artifacts, and helping his tribe recover stolen relics. Also, he joined the tribal drum group and wears his hair in very long braids. Todd got married and had four children. Their names are William, Daisy, Rainy and Lester. The beautiful and special Basket his great, great, great, great grandmother made sits in his dining room on the top shelf of the china cabinet.

This story is dedicated to all First Nations people out there who still are lost and trying to find their way. Whether it was due to boarding and residential schools, tribal displacement, alcohol and drugs, rejection, discrimination, hopelessness, fear, shame, poverty, or anything else. May you all find your path home.

⌘   ⌘   ⌘

The Crow

(In His Own Words)

I am the Crow,
Mystical as the Moon
And Dark as the Night,
Traversing through the Spirit World
On Shadow Wings of Flight.
Some have feared my Murky Hue,
Even called it a Curse,
But the Dimness of my Feathers,
Binds me to the Universe.
The Sun that you seek,
Is Beauty we cannot hide
The Glowing of my Feathers
Reflects the Light inside.
I'm the product of the Dream World,
Transformed by Creator's Gift,
Sometimes Bird,
Sometimes Man.
The Ability
To Shape–shift.
The things I Foresee,

Have Powerful Distinctions,
Like Earth, Fire, and Sky,
Guiding me to the Visions.
My Family Ties are Eternal and Strong,
Tight as a row of Corn,
Loving and Sharing with One Another,
From the moment we are Born.
My words have been misunderstood –
Sometimes, mistaken for a Caw,
But if you listen with your Heart:
I'm speaking Creator's Law.

Citrus Smile

Silent as the Breathing Wind-
Hushing of the tumbling Sea
Standing in the frozen sand,
Waiting,
For the visceral breeze.

The Omnipresent connection:
Traversing,
The Skin of the Earth-
Procreating- a mosaic of sound- and motion,
Cascading through time.
Undulation of Life and Death-
Counter flowing - in Symbiotic Love-
Enthralled,
In Harmonic Duality.

Closing my Eyes,
Taking flight -
Joined by the Ascending Air,
Revealing my Soul & Dreams to the Gale.

Listening to the Shaking Moon,
Weaving into the Stars-
Tasting your Citrus smile,
Reverberation of Healing & Warming Sand.
Unfurled Dust -
Tapestry of the Universe.

I've been here before

୧|୨

I've been here before,
Crackling whispers of the unfettered abyss,
Cold and gray as an arctic dawn.

Twisted flame and marrow on outstretched columns.
Vanishing flesh returning to the afterglow of memories.
Only the vultures have something nice to say.

Ah Yes,
I have been here.
Half eaten worms have joined forces to extricate the non-believers.
Sanity stored and hidden in the usual place.
Hidden to self, for itself.
Marveled by strangers scraping moon ash from their scales.

A Message
from Mother Earth

❀❀

To all my dear children:
I love you with all my heart.
But I get so sad-
They way you tear me apart.
You destroy my forests and pollute my seas,
You treat me like I was your worst enemy.
Poisoning my veins,
With mercury, lead, and toxic waste.
How could any Mother not be disgraced?
My own children have done this to me!
And you wonder why there is no harmony?
It took me billions of years-
To get this work done!
You damage me,
With just one revolution around Father Sun!
Earthquakes, hurricanes, and flooding rains,
Sorry to hurt you,
But these are the result of my pains.

Oh!

My Children!

Red, Black, Yellow, and White,

I wish you would take care of me as much as you fight.

Can't you see I have you revolve together?

So don't you think you should evolve together?

Because of my love,

I will suffer for you,

But it's harder to breathe,

While choking on black skies that should be blue.

So to all my little ones,

Love each other,

And take care of your Mother,

Because remember,

You won't have another.

Drove Past a
Funeral Home Today

ᏙᎤ

Drove past a funeral home today,
People standing outside,
Everyone dressed in black-
But not a single one cried.
Instead,
Their faces bounced with laughter-
Like hyenas over their prey,
Giddy at their morbid gathering,
Too happy-
I would say!
What could be so funny?
I thought as I drove up the hill,
Dead body inside,
Laying cold,
Empty and still.
Yes,
I've attended many funerals,
Where people smiled-

And seemed bright,
But there was something about-
The way they looked,
That just didn't feel right.
Maybe they weren't even humans,
But Reapers of the Dead,
Morphing into Sardonic Angels-
The moment I turned my head.

Dye for my Sin

ⓒ|ↄ

Ancient Seed of the Cosmic Dawn.
Premature growth causing a Race.
Running-
Against –
Creations-
Embrace.
Chasing Profits by the dozen.
Competing for the Superior Shade.
Disciples of the game scramble the Rules.
Like Black Yolk,
They Hatch intelligent confusion,
Weak Shells falling for the Cracks,
Fractured,
One over the Other,
Separated,
By Unequal Division.
The Universe is Swelling like a Bruise,
Revealing the sore Truth.
The Book is Black and Blue,
Abused and Misused,

As Pages turn Green.
Blood has hardened to my eyes-
& has made them like Stone.
A monument for the Vain,
Like Promises stabbed in the Sun.
The Narrow Void is darkened with the Stain,
Like the Path we were forced to Cross.
Dye me Human.
Survive for my Sins.
Color my Soul with the primordial Dust of the Sky.

Hearing Voices

Cataclysmic activity,
Crushes roots of lexicon formation.
Seismic scale-
Of toxic reverberation.
Syntax on pause-
Waiting for the solution.
Chaotic brainstorm,
Entombed-
Like neurotic pollution.
Bombastic waves-
Chew through chemical restraints,
Fending off the demons,
To save the pain for the saints.
In complete fear,
Of the verbal invasion,
Choosing the wrong dose
Leads to mind Castration.

I Love Pow Wow

೮ಿ೨

Beautiful Saturday morning,
Gonna have breakfast on the go,
We're hittin' the Pow Wow Trail,
Got 49 miles of road.
Regalia, Feathers and Drum
Packed gently.
Can't wait for the MC
To call, "Grand Entry!"
To see family and friends
Will be a delightful sight,
And that gorgeous Jingle Dress-
She finished sewing last night.
The sound of the drums,
Heart Beat of Mother Earth,
Dancers move in a circle-
Connecting with their birth.
Dancing for the Spirits,
As we move to the beat,
Touching Mother Earth,
We Pray with our Feet.

Honoring the Four-Legged and Winged,
Their Strength that we so admire,
Our movements tell their story,
As we go around the Sacred Fire.
The Drummers keep the rhythm,
Of the Ancient Voices of long ago,
Connecting with Earth and Sky,
The Eagle Whistle blows.
Every Dancer is in the Circle,
As we dance into the night
Colorful beads, shells and Feathers,
Seem to be taking flight!
The scent of sweetgrass and sage,
Softly blesses the lands,
Crafters, cooks, and vendors,
Serving laughter by their stands.
I love to Pow-Wow!
Its unity, love, and respect,
So please come and join us,
If you have not been here yet!

Shatter-Proof Heart

Shatter-proof heart;
Find your way home.
Hope is a sour dream-
That has rusted my bones.
The buzzing storms,
The aching thorns,
Blades of grass like piercing swords.
The burden of light,
The freedom of dark,
It's strange the way we have to depart.
Slipping like freedom,
Stained with drops of remorse;
Hollow tear drops follow their usual course.
Like fine music-
It is the Me in you I wish to Play.
Shatter-proof heart:
Find your way home.
I am in a dark corner,
Alone.

⌘ ⌘ ⌘

Edge of Sanity

❀

Contemplations strung together,
Hung on lines,
Of Devine Reality,
Or Temporal Illusion.
Choking on Malignant Memories,
Of The Nightmare,
Of life's Confusion.
I Cast out Nets and Traps,
In the Hope to Confine my Fears,
Even though the most Terrifying Place,
Is Ensnared between my Ears.
It makes a Slashing Escape,
Thrusting out my Fingers,
Leaving behind Black Stained Slime,
To ensure the Marks will Linger.
Elegant Scars,
Scripting my Soul,
A lovely Carving,
Like digging for Coal.
Suffocating Deep Inside,

I Crawl Lower,
Waiting for the Pain,
And the Horror to be Over.
I Turn into a Worm,
Or a Maggot to Escape with Wings,
But Nothing Changes,
Just Time on a String.

Heart in the Clouds

Heart in the clouds,
Traversing the fragmented sky –
The Binary Wind,
Forces the Earth to Cry.
Heart Burns down,
Like Tears of Ember,
Discharging from a departed plague-
Erupting from my Center.
Illuminating the Dreams,
Like diaphanous blood,
Cursed into existence-
And transfused from above.
Like a diffused kingdom,
And removed from my Throne,
Destitute in a dark place,
False comfort in the womb.
Clouds become Heartless,
And gather to Cheat the Sun,
Like a viscous path,
Crossed and Undone.

Downstairs Devil

❀

Took one last drag and polished off the soda before I walked to the door.
The door was cold as ice and rotten with moldy wood.

Slowly I pushed it open, inhaling cobwebs and dust as I walked in.
Immediately my eyes are pulled to the floor.

Vomit, blood and some unknown substances,
Splattered around like grease from Grungy's Chicken Shack®.

But it didn't smell like chicken fat at all.
The odor was much Fowler indeed.

More like decrepit melted flesh, urine, raw sewage and formaldehyde.
That's when I noticed the old tin can by the top of the basements stairs,

I move in for a closer look.
It had some human parts hanging over the side of it.

Then there was a trail of blood, entrails, and diet coke
leading down the stairs.
I slowly & carefully walk down the stairs,

Trying to hold on to the rail but it was slippery, layered
with blood and mucus.
Step by step I walked closer to what awaits,

The hairs on the back of my neck sticking up with nervous anticipation!
Finally, I'm in the basement!

Dreary and cold like an uncovered grave.
Not even my worst nightmares could conjure such calam-
ity and revulsion!

It was ten times worse than the scene upstairs!
An abominable display of the worst of human kind!

Then, I walked over to the little dirty and rusty refrigerator.
I slowly opened the door,

I looked inside and I'm startled with fright!
My heart and head dizzy with disgust,

Wincing and dry heaving,
I was mortified by what it revealed:
I was out of Diet Coke.

Wounded Rain

Wounded Rain
Bleeding from the descending pain.
Gray mist, clouded with charcoal stain.
Lonely vestiges, poor and pouring
Into the collecting swirl-
Seeking mercy-
In an unknown world.

Ejected from the Great Fountain,
With each drop -
We sharpen every Mountain.
The Torrential Traducer
Now plays his part,
Like splashing-up scars,
Exposing, the drenched heart.
Heavy as thirst,
Light as shadow,
A plunge seeking life,
In a lake gone shallow.

Cerulean Skies

ೞ

Cerulean Skies,
Interlaced With Fluffy Vanilla Bars,
Stretched out like a Welcome Mat
Leading to the Stars.
Cool breeze,
Kisses my skin,
Warmth from the Sun,
Flowing within.
As the charming Maple Tree waves Hello,
The budding green grass
Sparkles with a glow.
The Rows of Vibrant Flowers,
Smiling,
And Smelling Sweet,
Humming birds,
And Bumble Bees,
Are invited for a treat.
The Talking Brook,
Has an Inviting sound,
Precious-

Flowing Beverage,
Hosting-
The Flavor of Life,
All Around.
This is a Good Day,
A Pretty Day,
A Pretty Good Day.
The Kind of Day,
You give a Stranger a Hug,
So we can all take joy-
In the Equal Distribution of Love.

Madness

Twisted like a Lash and Castigated to my own Madness.
The Brutal verity that has impaled Motive to my Heart.
Clashing with the Wind and swallowing the Stones.
Unrefined message in the weight of Salt.
Hacked in two by the Dream-
And preserved with artificial Shadows.
Duplicity and She-
Have Scorned the Sun.
Vision raided -
By the Rapacious Burn.
Chilled with Pensive Remorse.
Cursing the Gravity,
And Waiting for the righteous Giant.

Garbage Eater

You love It!
Rancid and riddled,
Undigested,
Served on a griddle.
Regurgitation of baloney,
Splashing over the can,
Words crawl out,
Like spoiled and tainted ham.
They slither to our ears,
Like mutable leeching compost,
Spreading more verbal disease,
Than a raunchy talk show host.
So, I'm not interested,
In what you're serving.
If the truth was Ice,
Your tongue would be Burning.

Sneaking into
the Dream

◑◐

Hollow footsteps, heavy as stone but silent as death.
We go from this place, and then we are replaced.
Turning into the crumbled wave, drowning in decrepitude.
Breathing the milky Sun no more.
Now,
We are mesmerized by the burning moon, enchanted by
the stars in all their pointy reckoning.
The ecstasy of the thief; giddiness with unnatural
possession of time.
The glowing red hands, tainted with indigo of
smoldering shame.
Holding my breath, in fear of the descending smoke that
has embarrassed me all my nights.
Exhaling into the rancid flame, it's what we expected.
Setting free a smile like a caged animal.
Walking, running, now flying.

Professor Profess

❦

You have intellectual prowess,
According to the Billboard on your Wall,
But I think it's comparable, to other achievements-
Like something etched on a Bathroom Stall.
Very Disturbing -
For all the students, *Who Was Here* –
Having their Papers Wiped and Flushed,
And Ideas put to the Rear.
Your grading style is Degraded-
By your lack of Nuance, Creativity & Practical Application-
Treating Students like single minded robots,
Or Slaves on your personal plantation.
Knowledge should be a wondrous path-
A journey with Many Roads,
But because of your closed and narrow mind-
It becomes a Dead End with a hefty Toll.
Learning & **Teaching**,
Encompasses a Diverse Methodology –
However, your ridged lesson plans -
Lacks any Epistemology.

You should try getting outside yourself-
So the classroom is not about You!
Being forced to suffer through your Idiosyncrasies –
Is not the reason we came to School!
Sadly your best skill has been,
To convince some students that their insufficient,
Deducting 10 points here - and 10 points there-
For things - nothing to do with their commitment.
Your classroom Abounds-
With Dedication & Originality-
Don't be intimidated –
By- Cultural Plurality.
The second we believe-
We know it all-
Is the Second we Fail-
Because we put up a Wall.
You think your methods are faultless-
Your grading apocalyptic-
But when it comes to your students-
You remain pessimistic.
So Please- don't let the initials –
MBA, MEd, PhD -stop you from Thinking,
Because Just like words etched on a Bathroom Stall-
Any B.S. can start Stinking.

Melting Candle

Your Glow,
Is like a Blind,
Melting Candle,
Reflecting
Incandescent Madness,
Dissolving,
To a Coarse End.
Blistering,
Paraffin Tears,
Like liquefied Misery,
Hardened
Against you.
The Fading of the Flicker,
Preparing for a Dark Feast.
For You,
Shall nourish the Gloom.
Like Perverted Carrion,
Devoured and Defiled-
By your own Ruse.
Your murky appetite

Will illuminate your Sorrow –
With perfect Taste.
Your Waxing
Will Wane,
To host
Your Beleaguered
And disassembled Residue-
To A Final
And Deformed Crumb.
I watched the Candle Melt,
I watched,
From a prudent distance.
With Suspense,
But More Pity.
I tried once,
To unbend this crooked Flame,
Only to be reproached
In the Third Degree.
So I watch-
As the Candle Melts,
And when the fire hurls its final spark,
The agony shall begin.

Remove

Remove me from time, leave me in space and free my dreams.

My ear to the water, listening to the sublime chant.

Let the breathing Sun stir the shadows.

Another year upon the horizon, something new, waits in time.

Things never seen, said or heard before.

Third eye expectation fools thought and freedom.

Manufactured world tells us it's just a re-run, everyone becomes perplexed.

Everything is funny, everything is sad.

Matter only Matters to Matter.

Humans trying to fit into Matter

Obligatory routine drains the soul.

Take me to the edge where it's safe.

Quicken my sight with the vestal universe.

Being awake is frightening but it's so hard to go back to sleep.

The sleep keeps me from my dreams.

Lucid nightmares of linear reality.

One-dimensional ghosts casting plastic shadows.

Breathing is easy with no pressure.

Staying under water to slow down time.

Pressing to the womb

❦

Pressing to the womb, exit to false places in toy skies.
This is the year of the Shadow.

Trembling, as the gushing fluids push me past sordid monsters with bad attitudes.
One thought away from a sweet smell, one imagination from tranquil peace,

All while fettered to the bosom of the avarice beast.
Freedom comes at a fee of self-disconnection.

Drifting with all haste,
And put through the shredder and cast into the race.

The Blowing smile, cheated by the mourning tears.
Searching for the green remedy to cure the charcoal fears.

Each day, walking on the unbreakable mirror.
Who will crack first?

Fools Mask

The stolid charade
Observed by the gawking horde,
The pretentious buffoon keeping us all from being bored.
Yes, the corporal theatre is a prolific place,
Easy to fall of stage,
When blinded by a Canned Heat face.
You parade forward in your pathetic task,
Vomiting out platitudes while clutching to your mask.
The ostrich with its head in the sand,
And all those buried dreams,
You're like a horror picture show,
With all those bestial scenes.
We all reflect back,
When you had sure vision,
Now your sight has been cheated,
By your self made collision.
Reaching out to your aid,
Which you shunned with great haste;
Like a baby sucking to the breast,
You swallow shamelessly with no waste.

No more jokes-
Only a myriad of tears,
You wear you fools mask so proud...
Looks like you'll be keeping it for years.

The Hateful Look

At last,
Razor-laced eyes,
Used to cut through the snorting Sun
And fill the last vestige of life.

All traces of humanity oozing out unto the old wooden
and splinter infested floor,
    Limping down the gravity trail,
    Tasting cob webs and moss laden cracks.

The explication of Meaning, the antithesis of nothing;
The prelude to the precursor.
Spiraling in and out of control,
What a beautiful site,
Makes you cough up seeds of delight.

Choking on reality smog.
Melted dreams screaming into the bloody mirror –
With glances of implication and arousal,
Like a path of blue powder leading to the mud-filled
cage.
Now I know what it's all about,
Eat or be eaten,
In the time honored plague of descending beauty,
Could it be that simple?

The Darkening

Shhhh,
Be Still.
It's Time.
The Reverse Sun is pulling back from the Trees.
Light is Shrinking like a drying Leaf-
And dragging away Memories like Powder-
To Season the Sky with Dreams.
I've turned Inside Out to Undo the Paths.
The Visible Wounds are easy to Heal.
Like a Collapsed Star,
Keeping the Pressure Within,
Avoiding the Sting-
Through the Shortcut in the Night.
The Roads Canceled of my Steps.
Too Heavy to Travel Above,
Too much Light to leave a Trace.
My Basket is Empty with the Weight of the World.
Walking backward to Free Time,
But it was never mine to Keep.

My Words
Mean Nothing

◑◑

Transmutation of my Voice,
My words mean Nothing.
I'm just the Dust in the Dark,
Like a Forest crying Red.
The Storm has captured my Fever,
Like a Rainbow casting Shadow.
These are the Days measured by Sound.
The Wind completes the Circle,
With the caressing Echoes of Harmony.
The Language of Light,
Kissing the Air.
Breathe...
The Untouchable Force,
Steadying my Tongue.
I'm Inside the Flame.
I disperse with every Flicker,
Sparks of a Dream to ignite the Flow.
Unconscious Waves make their return,

Like Iron lips pounding the Shores.
These are the Nights, that Pulsate recollection,
Like the whispering Heart, singing to the Moon.
My Words mean nothing.
I'm just a haze in Time,
Like fog, Fading into the Rain.
A Requiem for Ghosts,
Daring to Speak.

⌘　⌘　⌘

Acknowledgments

I want to first sincerely thank Donna (Laurent) Caruso for all the wonderful help she provided. This being my first book, I was not sure where best to find an editor. Donna, understanding my situation, did not hesitate to help me through this process and believed in my work. She is truly a gem of a person and I can't thank her enough. Also, a special and BIG thanks to the Award Winning director and producer Chris Eyre for taking time to review my work. And thank you Chris for taking Indian Country to the entire world with your amazing films and other works.

Kuttabatimish! (Thank You Very Much!) Lisa Brooks, Assistant Professor of History and Literature and of Folklore and Mythology, Harvard University. Your time and advice has been a precious resource.

Thanks to Ron Welburn, author, poet and Professor of English and Native American Studies at the University of Massachusetts, Amherst: A deep and heartfelt thanks, not only for reviewing my work but for always being out there in the Sacred Circle as an Elder and Keeper of the Traditions.

Thank you Michelle Vigeant for your beautiful artwork! Finding you was a serendipitous event. While sitting in class daydreaming about where I could find an artist for my cover, there was a girl sketching next to me. When I asked her about her work, she replied, "Do you really want to meet somebody good? I'll introduce you to my sister." And thus began the process of our collaboration. Your work has captured the visceral image I wanted to present for this book. Well done!

Kuttabatimish Amber Rubidoux for the great photos! It was a little cold that day but nonetheless we had a great shoot and I appreciate your time.

To my Ancestors in the Spirit World: I thank you and honor you. I pray that in some small way this work will transcend the pages and provoke a higher consciousness of who we are and demonstrate that our story is more than that of one about the past but also about a future that is still being created and reborn with every generation that comes. *Kuttabatimish* to all my Nipmuc Elders. Thank you for being the guiding force and leaving behind the stories and good words to guide our people. To All Nipmuck people: I hope this book will make you all proud because I'm certainly proud to be one of you. Thank you, I love you all! Thank You – Thank You! To all my friends, family and the people that have touched my life along this journey.

Special thanks to all of you who choose to pick up a copy of *Tales from the Whispering Basket*. I am humbled and honored to share my stories and words with you.

To my Mom, Grandma and Grandpa; thank you for keeping those traditional stories in the family alive. You always taught us who we are. Thanks. Love you! To my four children, Manixit, Anoki, Nantai, and Nathalie: I love you guys so much; you have blessed my life and have been with me on the powwow trail since your birth. What a beautiful journey it has been! I'm honored to be your father. Ah, and my wife, Licy. There are not enough pages to tell of the joy it's been being your husband. You have given me more than I could ever imagine. You are such a special, beautiful and multi-talented person. I love you, darling!

Larry Spotted Crow Mann

CPSIA information can be obtained
at www.ICGtesting.com
Printed in the USA
BVHW041448261120
594285BV00018B/104